Medieval Manuscripts
In the Norlin Library
& the Department of Fine Arts
at the University of Colorado at Boulder

A *Summary Catalogue*

Medieval Manuscripts
In the Norlin Library
& the Department of Fine Arts
at the University of Colorado at Boulder

A Summary Catalogue

Compiled by
Julia Boffey & A.S.G. Edwards

In collaboration with
Melody Fields, B. G. Harding, & Dana Symons

Incorporating contributions from
Paula Balafas, Ruth Feiertag, Jana Matthews,
Katherine Millersdaughter, Benjamin Perry,
Angela Sucich, Katherine Steele, & Amy Vines

Pegasus Press
FAIRVIEW, NORTH CAROLINA
2002

Pegasus Press
PO BOX 2265
FAIRVIEW NC 28730

This book is made to last.
It is set in Palatino and Carolina,
and printed on acid-free paper
to library specifications.

Printed in the United States of America.

TABLE OF CONTENTS

The plates follow the indices.

PREFACE

This Summary Catalogue has its origins in a graduate course in palaeography given by Julia Boffey and A.S.G. Edwards in the summer of 1998 under the auspices of the Center for British Studies at the University of Colorado at Boulder. This led to the first systematic examination of the medieval manuscript holdings of the University Libraries. A substantial number of descriptions of manuscripts were drafted during this course. Subsequently three students, Melody Fields, B.G. Harding, and Dana Symons, drafted further descriptions and undertook additional research. The specific contributions of all these students are acknowledged in those entries after which their initials appear in the catalogue. Boffey and Edwards returned to Boulder in the summer of 2000 to work with these students on revising the draft descriptions and adding ones for those manuscripts not previously described and/ or which had subsequently come to light. It is the work of all these students that has provided much of the material for this catalogue; we owe a great deal to their energy, enthusiasm, and scholarship.

We all owe a great debt to the Heads of Special Collections in the University Libraries with whom we have worked, Susan Thach Dean and Deborah Hollis, and to members of their staff, especially Kris McCusker and Chris Vincent whose enthusiasm and knowledge have made our work far simpler – and more pleasurable. In the later stages of our work Michelle Visser of Special Collections has given much additional assistance, as has Courtney

Wennerstrom of the Center for British Studies. Bridget A. Carlin, Collection Manager, Colorado Collection, Department of Fine Arts, has been generous in providing access to and information about manuscript leaves under her care. James F. Williams II, Dean of Libraries at the University of Colorado at Boulder, has lent support throughout and provided generous funding. We are also grateful for similarly generous funding support to the President's Fund for the Humanities, the Arts and Sciences Development Fund, the Greenlee Family Foundation, the Friends of the Libraries, and the Center for British Studies.

The Special Collections Department would also like to thank the following people who have substantially contributed to building the collection and assisting in the preparation of this catalogue. Without them, there would be no collection: Ellsworth Mason, formerly Special Collections Department Head, who acquired the S. Harrison Thomson Collection, and other leaves making up almost one-fourth of the whole collection; Nora Quinlan, during whose time as Head of the Special Collections Department the majority of the collection was acquired, and who staged several displays of the collection; Liesel Nolan, Head of the Art and Architecture Library, who was instrumental in the purchase of manuscripts; Carol Klemme, formerly Acting Head of Special Collections, when a number of manuscripts were purchased; Susan Thorning, University of Colorado Foundation, for much assistance in obtaining funds for the preparation of the catalogue. Other contributions are acknowledged under the specific collections or manuscripts with which they are associated, but particular thanks are due to Diane and Robert Greenlee. Their acts of generosity are recorded elsewhere but they have been a constant support to the work of the Special Collections Department.

We also express our gratitude for kind assistance to Professor Virginia Brown, Dr Lisa Fagin Davis, Dr A.I. Doyle, Dr Consuelo Dutschke, Peter Kidd, Richard Linenthal, Professor Fred Porcheddu, Dr Barbara Shailor, and Dr Kay Sutton. We owe a particular debt to Dr Christopher de Hamel, Fellow and Librarian of Corpus

Christi College, Cambridge, and formerly Head of the Department of Western Manuscripts at Sotheby's. Not only has he commented on and made additions and corrections to parts of this catalogue, but his sale catalogue descriptions have always been vital tools of unobtrusive scholarship and have provided the only secure guide through the maze of manuscript fragments with which we have had to deal. We are also most grateful to the many librarians who have answered our questions about manuscripts in their care.

In the final stages of our work, we benefitted from the keen eye of Darlene Hollingsworth, who spotted a number of omissions and inconsistencies. Beth McDonald copy-edited a difficult manuscript with calm intelligence. Words cannot convey what we owe to Mario Di Cesare, our publisher. His scholarship, enthusiasm, and focus are the main reasons that this book has appeared.

Our greatest debt is to Professor Elizabeth Robertson, Director of the Center for British Studies, who planned the original graduate course out of which this catalogue grew, and whose subsequent efforts have ensured its completion. We are all conscious of the example of selfless commitment to an idea of scholarship that she embodies. As colleagues and former students we acknowledge how much we owe her.

This catalogue has been published in time for the biennial meeting of the New Chaucer Society held at Boulder in July 2002. In conjunction with this meeting an exhibition of selected medieval manuscripts and leaves is to be held in the Special Collections Department of the University Libraries. We hope that the conjunction of these two events will enhance awareness of the range of medieval manuscripts at the University of Colorado at Boulder.

JULIA BOFFEY
A.S.G. EDWARDS

ix

Introduction

This Summary Catalogue lists all the medieval manuscript holdings in the University of Colorado at Boulder (UCB), that is, those
in the Special Collections Department of the University Libraries
and in the Library of the Colorado Collection of the Department
of Fine Arts. The libraries' holdings encompass four distinct
collections: Miscellaneous Manuscripts, comprising currently
forty–three separate manuscripts or fragments; the Otto Ege
portfolio containing forty–five single leaves; the relevant portions
of the James Hayes collection, fifty–two separate items, some
comprising more than one leaf; and the collection of medieval
fragments formed by S. Harrison Thomson, forty–four separate
manuscript items. In addition, we have included seven leaves in
the Colorado Collection of the Department of Fine Arts at UCB.

The collecting of medieval manuscripts in any systematic
way has a fairly recent history at UCB. Some manuscripts (**MS 1,
MS 80, MS 102**) and occasional leaves (for example, **MS 334 OS**)
seem to have been acquired in the 1950s, but none appear in the
Supplement to de Ricci's *Census* (1962). Systematic acquisitions
were not made until the late 1970s or early 1980s with the acquisition of the S. Harrison Thomson collection of fragments (the
precise date of this acquisition cannot be established; it falls
sometime between 1973–1982). Other collections of leaves were
also subsequently purchased en bloc: the Otto Ege portfolio, *Fifty
Original Leaves from Medieval Manuscripts,* in 1989, and the James
Hayes collection in 1994. In addition, during the 1980s and 1990s

the Miscellaneous Manuscripts collection was developed through the purchase of individual items. An important figure in the impetus to such collecting was John Feldman, a local resident and collector, who gave or sold more than thirty manuscripts or leaves to UCB. Mention should also be made here of Dr Amy Vandersall, formerly of the Department of Fine Arts, who was one of the first scholars at UCB to urge the acquisition of medieval manuscripts and who was herself a donor to the library's collection.

The overwhelming majority of the manuscripts at UCB are single leaves or groups of leaves. There are, however, some notable complete manuscripts among the Miscellaneous Manuscripts collection, particularly **MS 299** and **300**, both thirteenth-century Paris Latin Bibles, with programmes of illustration, particularly extensive in the case of the former; the collection also includes a fourteenth-century Italian pseudo Augustine (**MS 1**), an Italian devotional work (**MS 102**), a French Book of Hours (**MS 313**), and an Italian manuscript of Horace (**MS 344**). The fragments offer a representative chronological range of the development of the manuscript book from the ninth century (**MS 355**) to the end of the Middle Ages. In its totality the collection is of great value for teaching purposes and contains a number of items of considerable intrinsic importance.

The catalogue itself aims to give, in as concise a form as possible, a systematic account of the content and physical form of each manuscript. There are limitations on what it has proved possible to achieve. The lack of systematic early library records has made the history of some acquisitions particularly obscure. Since many entries are for single leaves some effort has been made (under 'Provenance') to locate related leaves or groups of leaves. Clearly more work remains to be done in this respect, and we would welcome further information. Equally clearly, a number of leaves require more precise identification and/or localization. But in spite of the limits on what has proved possible we hope this work will serve to make scholars conscious of the extent of the medieval manuscript holdings at UCB.

The initial draft of each description was prepared by the person whose initials appear in bold in parentheses at the end. All descriptions were revised and edited by Boffey and Edwards. They are responsible for any unsigned descriptions in their entirety and for all remaining errors.

CONTRIBUTORS

AS	Angela Sucich
AV	Amy Vines
BGH	B. G. Harding
BP	Benjamin Perry
DS	Dana Symons
JM	Jana Matthews
KM	Katherine Millersdaughter
KS	Katherine Steele
MF	Melody Fields
PB	Paula Balafas
RF	Ruth Feiertag

Summary Catalogue

Miscellaneous Manuscripts

The term 'Miscellaneous' denotes the library's individual acquisitions, mainly from the late 1980s onwards, though some materials were acquired prior to that period, at dates that seem impossible to establish with certainty.

MS 1: Pseudo Augustine, *Meditations* (ff. 1–31v); *Soliloquies* (ff. 32–49); *Manuale … de verbo domini* (ff. 50–61v); *De fide ad Petrum* (ff. 62–64v). Venice, late s. xv. 180 x 124 mm. Paper. Ff. 71.

Single column; 140 x 80 mm.; 36 lines; ruled and bounded in plummet. Red and black 2-line initials; some rubrication.

Collation: a–e^8, f^8 (wanting), [g]–[h]^8, i^8, [k]^8 (text ends fol. 64v rest of gathering blank).

Provenance: Bought from H. P. Kraus at an unknown date, but probably in the 1950s.

MS 80: *Distinctiones evangeliorum*. Italy, s. xiii. 188 x 126 mm. Parchment. Ff. 295.

Double column; each column 125/30 x 45 mm.; ruled and bounded in drypoint. Blue or red painted initials with some pen-work decoration on fols. 1–58; similar kinds of blue initials in the rest of the manuscript, but with more elaborate decoration.

The contents of the manuscript are: (i) a set of distinctions in 117 chapters headed 'distinctiones euangeliorum' ending with distinctions to do with the seven deadly sins (fols. 1–54v), followed (fols. 54v–57) by a further, unidentified text in a different hand; (ii) another set of 'distinctiones euangeliorum' in 185 chapters in another hand.

Collation: 1^{12}, 2^{14} (wants 1 leaf), $3-4^{12}$, 5^8; 6^{10}, $7-9^{12}$, 10^{10}, $11-25^{12}$; catchwords from gathering 6 (fol. 69v).

Originally seemingly two separate MSS, (i) constituting the first five quires (fols. 1–58); (ii) fols. 59–295.

Provenance: Bought from Libreria Antiquaria Morelli, Catalogue 18 (1956), no. 17, for 20,000 lire.

MS 102: *Esposizione degli Evangeli*. Tuscany, c. 1350–1400. 290 x 220 mm. Paper. Ff. 147 + i.

Double column; each column 200 x 80 mm.; 30–32 lines to a column. Blue and red painted initials (2-line); frequent rubrication.

Collation: 1^{12} (wants 1, probably blank), $2-12^{12}$, 13^4; catchwords.

Provenance: Bought from Alan Thomas in 1973.

Pl. 3   **MS 284**: Latin Bible, New Testament (2 Corinthians 12: 4 – Galatians 2: 6). France, s. xiii². 146 x 105 mm. Parchment. Single leaf.

Double column; each column 102 x 30 mm.; 50 lines to a column; ruled and bounded in plummet. Historiated initial *P* (figure of man falling off horse) in blue, pink, white, and black on recto; also decorated *O*, *E*, and *F*; elaborate blue and red penworked initial *E* on verso.

Provenance: Bought by Ferrini from Heritage Books and broken up (the circumstances of its dismemberment ex inf. John Feldman, 1 November 1999). See also leaves **285**, **291**, **319**, and Department of Fine Arts **MS 86.1911P**, for others from this MS at UCB. Purchased by John Feldman (his MS 12). Gift of Feldman to UCB, 12 February 1990. Other leaves from the same MS:

    (i)   two leaves, Schuster Gallery, *Illuminated Manuscripts* (London, 1987), nos. 8–9;

    (ii) one leaf, Sotheby's, 17 December 1991, lot 13;

    (iii) two leaves, Ferrini, Catalogue 1 (1987), nos. 12–13.

A number of other single leaves are noted in Lynda Ericson Bair, 'Evidence of Production of Thirteenth-Century Pocket Bibles,' MA thesis, University of Colorado, 1991, Appendix 1, nos. 4–10:
(i) Pirages, Catalogue 9, items 9–10: both unsold and returned to consignor;
(ii) Pirages, Catalogue 12, item 12;
(iii) Edward R. Lubin, *European Illuminated Manuscripts*, Catalogues 8–11; it has not proved possible to obtain more information about these leaves. (**KS**)

Pl. 3   **MS 285**: Latin Bible, New Testament (1 Timothy 6: 4 – 2 Timothy 3: 1). France, s. xiii². 146 x 105 mm. Parchment. Single leaf.

Double column; each column 102 x 30 mm.; 50 lines to a column; ruled and bounded in plummet. Historiated initial *P* (11-line) incorporating two male figures, one nimbed and assisting the other. Outlines in margin in plummet, possibly drafts for this initial.

Provenance: Bought from Ferrini by John Feldman (ex inf. John Feldman, 1 November 1999); his MS 13. Purchased from Feldman by UCB, 12 February 1990 for $3,900; see further **MS 284**. (**MF**)

Pl. 7   **MS 287**: Latin Bible (Lamentation 5: 11 – Baruch 2: 21). France (?), s. xiii (?). 187 x 129 mm. Parchment. Single leaf.

Double column; each column 122 x 38 mm.; 32 lines to a column; ruled and bounded in ink. Historiated initial *C* (6-line) on recto at beginning of Baruch, depicting Baruch as a seated figure in green and red holding a scroll, attached to a demi-vinet border dividing the columns; another extends the length of the inner border with a 3-line illuminated initial.

Provenance: Gift of John Feldman and Jenni Inman to UCB, 15 October 1990 in memory of William Wallace Carson. (**KM**)

MS 291: Latin Bible (1 Maccabees 1: 1 – 2: 14). France, s. xiii². 146 x 105 mm. Parchment. Single leaf.

Double column; each column 102 x 30 mm.; 50 lines to a column; ruled and bounded in plummet. Historiated *E* (9-line) on recto, portraying the beheading of the idolatrous Jew.

Provenance: '368' in pencil on bottom right hand recto. Sold Sotheby's, 17 December 1991, part of lot 13. Purchased from Maggs, 30 April 1992 for £1,000; see further **MS 284**. (**KM**)

MS 299: Latin Bible. France (Paris), 1240–50. 180 x 122 mm. Parchment. Ff. 602.

Double column; each column 110 x 40 mm.; 41 lines to a column.

Collation: i–xiv^{24}, xv^{22}, xvi–xxiii^{24}, xxiv^{10}, xxv^{22}, xxvi ^{24} (wants 3 leaves); some catchwords, signatures; contemporary foliation, but with numbers '370–399' omitted (the break comes at the end of a quire, but without loss of text); numbering stops at '501' after which there are forty-two unnumbered leaves. Eighty-two historiated initials (between 7–32 lines), fols. 1 (St. Jerome), 5, 28 (God and Moses), 47v (priests sacrificing at altar), 60v (God and Moses), 78v (Moses with tablets), 96 (Joshua), 107 (Joshua with an angel), 118v (Elimelech and Naomi), 121 (death of sons of Eli), 136v (David and the Amalekite), 149 (Abishag and David), 164 (Ahaziah), 178v (Adam's descendants), 191v (Solomon), 207v (Cyrus), 212 (Nehemiah), 218v (man at altar), 225 (Tobit), 229v (Judith and Holofernes), 235v (Esther, Ahasuerus, and Haman), 241v (Job on a dung heap), 252v (David), 256v (Samuel and David), 259 (David), 261v (fool), 264 (David), 267 (David), 269v (two monks), 272v (God enthroned), 278v (Solomon and Rehoboam), 288 (Solomon), 291v (Virgin and Child), 293 (Solomon), 300v (Ecclesia), 319v (Isaiah), 342 (Jeremiah), 369 (Baruch), 401v (Ezechiel), 425v (Daniel), 435v (Hosea and Gomer), 439 (Joel), 441 (Amos), 443v (God and Obadiah), 444 (Jonah), 445 (Micah and God), 447 (Nahum), 448 (Habbakuk), 449v (Zephania), 450v (Haggai), 451v (Zachariah), 455v (Malachai), 457v (idolatrous Jew), 471v (messenger delivering letter), 495v (St. Mark), 504v (St. Luke), 519v (St. John), 532 (St. Paul), 537v (St. Paul), 542v (St.

Paul), 546 (St. Paul), 547v (St. Paul), 549v (St. Paul), 551 (St. Paul), 552 (St. Paul), 553 (St. Paul), 554 (St. Paul), 555v (St. Paul), 556v (St. Paul), 557 (St. Paul), 557v (St. Paul), 558v (St. Paul), 561v (St. Paul), 576v (St. James), 578 (St. Peter), 579v (St. Peter), 580v (St. John), 582 (St. John: two), 582v (St. Jude), 583 (St. John). Seventy-five blue painted initials, with red penwork (between 3–8 lines); blue and red painted border running the length of columns.

Provenance: 'iste liber pertinet frater Stephano Arundele, lectori in theologa ordinis fratrum beatissime de genetricis Marie de Monte Carmeli provincie Marie de Monte Carmeli provincie Sienne et conuentus Parisiensis' (partly legible only under ultra-violet); sold Sotheby's, 6 December 1988, lot 31 (with plate), to Fogg from whom Feldman purchased it in December 1988 (his MS 4); sold by him to UCB, 24 February 1994 for $50,000.

Pl. 15 **MS 300**: Latin Bible. France (Paris), s. xiii. 164 x 110 mm. (cropped). Parchment. Ff. 616 (misnumbered for 611 leaves).

Double column; each column 115 x 37 mm.; 49 lines to a column.

Collation: 1^{24}, 2^{28}, subsequently not determinable because of the tightness of the binding (however, the collation as reported in the Ferrini Catalogue below seems incorrect). Seven historiated initials, fols. 1 (St. Jerome), 4 (Seven Days of Creation: misnumbered '2'), 257v (David), 288 (Solomon), 329v (Isaiah), 457 (Matthew), 509v (Paul), illuminated initials (between 6–10 lines); painted initials (blue or red with contrasting penwork, 2–7 lines).

Provenance: A product of the so-called Soissons atelier, on which see Branner, pp. 77–78; Swann Galleries, New York, 4 May 1978, lot 23; Ferrini, Catalogue 1 (1987), no. 8 (with plate), to Feldman in July 1987; his MS 3; sold by him to UCB, 24 February 1994 for $30,000. Purchased with the Humanities Special Purchase Fund.

MS 308: Book of Hours (from Penitential Psalms). France, early s. xiv. 137 x 86 mm. Parchment. Single leaf.

Single column; 81 x 56 mm.; 20 lines; ruled and bounded in ink. Antlered and bearded animal outlined in ink, with body and antlers in gray/light blue, on recto as bottom line filler; another similar animal is first line filler on verso.

Provenance: Pencilled folio number '89' on recto. Gift of John Feldman to UCB, 14 December 1995. (**DS**)

Pl. 2 **MS 309**: Latin Bible, Old Testament (Psalm 51: 1–9, with commentary). France, s. xiii². 215 x 222/27 mm. (lower portion of leaf cut away). Parchment. Single leaf.

Double column; each column 188 x 75 mm.; 46 lines to a column; ruled in ink. Historiated initial *Q* depicting king and devil in blue, green, and red on recto. Naked white bearded figure between columns on verso. Frequent blue and red penwork initials.

Provenance: This leaf has been associated with productions of the so-called Almagest Atelier manuscripts, illuminated in or around Paris in the early thirteenth century, and typified in a manuscript of Ptolemy's Almagest made in 1213 (now BN lat. 16200); the atelier seems to have been responsible for the production of a number of pocket Bibles; see Branner, pp. 27–29 + fig. 24 and pp. 201–2 for a full list of related manuscripts; Christopher de Hamel, *A History of Illuminated Manuscripts* (London, 1986), p. 110 and plate 105. Purchased by John Feldman from D. Proski (Amsterdam) who had it from 'a Dutch collector' (details of provenance from Feldman, 1 November 1999). Gift of Feldman to UCB, November 1994. (**KS**)

Pl. 13 **MS 313**: Book of Hours. France, late s. xv. 144 x 101 mm. Parchment. Ff. 87 + i.

Single column; 100 x 60 mm.; 25 lines; ruled in ink. Pricking visible in outer margins. Large painted miniatures with borders, fols. 7, 36, 40, 49, 63 (the last two incorporating coats of arms); other painted initials in varying styles and sizes, but the majority in blue or red.

Collation: 1^8 (wants 8), 2^8 (wants 8), 3^8 (wants 2–7), 4^8 (wants

1–7), 5^8, 6^{10} (wants 6), $8–12^8$, 13^8 (wants 1); some catchwords. Large, crude painted miniatures with border on fols. 7 (Annunciation), 36 (St. Gregory), 40 (David in prayer), 49 (Job on dung heap), 63 (Crucifixion), the last two incorporating coats of arms; other painted initials in varying styles and sizes, the majority blue or red. In a limp vellum binding.

Provenance: Swann Galleries to Alan Culton (a Boulder dealer); sold by him c. 1984/85 to Feldman (details of provenance from Feldman, 1 November 1999); given by him to UCB in September 1986.

Pl. 2 **MS 314**: Latin Bible (Leviticus 26: 26 – Numbers 1: 19). Northern France (?), early s. xiii. 443 x 303 mm. Parchment. Single leaf.

Double column; each column 312 x 98 mm.; 22 lines to a column; ruled and bounded; prick marks in inner margin. Large historiated *L* on verso (beginning of Numbers), extending above the top column margin and into the gap between columns, of double-headed dragon in pink, blue, and white; 5-line initial *L* with red and blue penwork ornamentation on recto.

Provenance: Purchased from L. Witten, *Early English Manuscripts and Illuminated Leaves*, Catalogue 12 (1980), no. 41, for $4,000. (**MF**)

MS 315: Book of Hours (possibly from the Suffrages). Southern Netherlands, c. 1435. 148/51 x 111 mm. Parchment. Two leaves.

Single column; ruled and bounded in faded red ink; number of lines and size of text block varies. One leaf has a large miniature of St. Eustace in a gilt frame with a full-page border of foliate decoration with a 3-line illuminated initial *G*, infilled in blue, red, and gold, on a gold ground. The other leaf has several 2-line gilt initials, infilled in blue or red with white tracery on a blue or purple ground; some rubrication.

Provenance: Bought by John Feldman at the California Book Fair in Los Angeles, c. 1980 (details of provenance from Feldman, 1 November 1999). Gift of Feldman to UCB in 1986. (**MF**)

Pl. 1 **MS 316**: Cutting. Paris, 1210–20. 185 x 42 mm. (at widest point). Parchment.

Historiated initial, possibly an *F*, from the words 'Frater Ambrosius' which begin St. Jerome's letter to Bishop Paulinus, normally prefacing Genesis in the medieval Bible. It depicts a seated man offering a book to a kneeling man; tail of letter is zoomorphic, including a figure with the head of a lion, or dog, with wings and birdlike feet.

Provenance: Bought by Ferrini from the Mortimer Brandt Collection, MS 1298–12; see Harry Bober, *Miniatures from Illuminated Manuscripts: The Mortimer Brandt Collection* (Brooks Memorial Gallery, Memphis, TN, 1966), pp. 9–11 + plate 4; bought by John Feldman from Ferrini in November 1988; his MS 8. Co-purchased by Special Collections Department and Fine Arts Bibliographer Liesel Nolan, 24 September 1991 for $5,000. (**KS**)

Pl. 7 **MS 317**: Latin Bible (Jerome, Prologue to Job – Job 5: 9). Paris, c. 1220–30. 256 x 173 mm. Parchment. Single leaf.

Double column; each column 167 x 46 mm.; 57 lines to a column; ruled and bounded in plummet; prick marks in inner margin.

Historiated blue initial *U* (10-line), on verso, at beginning of Book of Job, depicting naked, diseased Job on dung heap, with his wife, three sons, and the devil, within a gilt frame. Illuminated initial *S* (8-line), also on verso, containing zoomorphic shapes, within a gilt frame.

Provenance: Bought by John Feldman from Quaritch, March 1988 for $3,500; his MS 6. Purchased by UCB, April 1991 from him for $5,000. From the same manuscript as **MS 318**. Other leaves from this MS include:
    (i)   two leaves, Sotheby's, 2 December 1997, lot 48 (with plate) from the collection of Neil Phillips (MS 791);
    (ii) one leaf, Quaritch, Catalogue 1270 (2000), no. 18. (**BGH**)

Pl. 7 **MS 318**: Latin Bible (Leviticus 46: 11 – Jerome's Prologue to Daniel). Paris, c. 1220–30. 257 x 170 mm. Parchment. Single leaf.

Double column; each column 170 x 98 mm.; 55 lines to a column; ruled and bounded in plummet; prick marks in inner margin. Historiated initial *D* on verso (beginning of Daniel), of two entwined dragons, red, blue, and green, whose tails form a knot design.

Provenance: From the Almagest atelier (on which see **MS 309**). Bought by John Feldman from Quaritch, March 1988 for $2,250; his MS 7. Purchased by UCB, April 1991 for $2,500. From the same manuscript as **MS 317**. (**MF**)

MS 319: Latin Bible (Luke 6: 35 – 7: 44). France, s. xiii². 146 x 105 mm. Parchment. Single leaf.

Double column; each column 102 x 30 mm.; 50 lines to a column; ruled and bounded in plummet.

Provenance: Purchased from Pirages, Catalogue 26, no. 2, 22 June 1993 for $150; see further **MS 284**. (**MF**)

Pl. 5 **MS 320**: Latin Bible, Old Testament (Psalm 144: 21 – Proverbs 1: 1). Paris, c. 1250–75. 232 x 157 mm. Parchment. Single leaf.

Double column; each column 162 x 48 mm.; 51 lines to a column; ruled and bounded in plummet. Historiated *P* on verso, depicting Solomon instructing his son Rehoboam, on a blue frame with a diapered pattern of squares and diamonds in light blue and rust. Large illuminated *I* on verso and other smaller illuminated initials on recto.

Provenance: Attributed to the atelier of the Dominican Painter (on whom see Branner, pp. 118–22). A leaf from a MS formerly in the collection of Sir Chester Beatty, his W. MS 116; see *Illuminated Manuscripts from the Library of Sir Chester Beatty* (Dublin, 1955), no. 10; sold Sotheby's, 3 December 1968, lot 14 when it comprised 187 (out of an original 549) leaves and subsequently broken up:

(i)   one leaf, Sotheby's, 14 December 1977, lot 9 (to Maggs);
(ii)   four leaves, Sotheby's, 19 June 1979, lots 15–17;
(iii)   one leaf, Sotheby's, 3 July 1984, lot 3;

(iv)   five leaves, Sotheby's, 25 June 1985, lot 90;

(v)   two leaves, Sotheby's, 23 June 1987, lot 6;

(vi)   one leaf, Sotheby's, 19 June 1990, lot 47(2);

(vii)   one leaf, Sotheby's, 18 June 1991, lot 7;

(viii)   four leaves, Sotheby's, 21 June 1993, lot 7 (Alan Thomas sale);

(ix)   eight leaves, Sotheby's, 1 December 1998, lot 71;

(x)   one leaf, Alan Thomas, Catalogue 22, no. 1;

(xi)   two leaves, Alan Thomas, Catalogue 23, nos. 21–22;

(xii)   four leaves, Folio Fine Arts Catalogue 63 (May 1969), nos. 761–64;

(xiii)   twelve leaves, H. P. Kraus, Catalogue 188 (1991), no. 8;

(xiv)   two leaves, in the collection of William B. Edelman, his MSS 43, 48.

Provenance: Bought by John Feldman, June 1988; his MS 16. Purchased by UCB, April 1991 for $2,000. MS 320 seems to be one of the two leaves that formed Sotheby's, 19 June 1979, lot 15. (**AV**)

Pl. 1   **MS 321**: Cutting from Peter Lombard, *Commentary on Galatians.* Paris, c. 1230–40. Parchment.

Single illuminated initial *P* (6-line) on verso, in blue and red, touched with white, infilled with stems and flowers in pink, green, white, and blue, in a gilt frame marking beginning of commentary. Fragments of text on recto from preceding Commentary on 2 Corinthians.

Provenance: From the atelier of Gautier Lebaube (see Branner, pp. 72–75 and figs. 144–47); sold Sotheby's, 2 December 1986, lot 6(iii) to Ferrini for £352. Schuster Gallery, *Illuminated Manuscripts* (London, 1987), p. 15, no. 3; bought by John Feldman, March 1988; his MS 10. Purchased by UCB April 1991 for $950.

MS 322: Book of Hours. France (?), England (?), late s. xv. 174 x 136 mm. Parchment. Single leaf.

Single column; 99 x 70 mm.; 13 lines. Illuminated *O* (2-line) on red and blue ground, infilled with white and gray tracery.

Provenance: Pencilled on bottom recto: '32–152–8 $75'. (**DS**)

MS 323: Latin Bible (beginning of letter from Jerome to Bishop Paulinus, preceding Genesis). France (?), England (?), s. xiii. 199 x 150 mm. Parchment. Single leaf.

Double column; each column 153 x 47 mm.; 50 lines to a column; ruled and bounded in drypoint. 10-line painted initial *I* at beginning of letter, with descender extending the length of the inner margin (heavily oxidized); painted initial *F* on recto; initial *I* of same size.

Provenance: Obtained by John Feldman from Ferrini, c. 1988/89 (details of provenance from Feldman, 1 November 1999). Donated to UCB by Feldman, April 1991. (**BP**)

MS 324: Latin Bible (part of Jerome's *Preface*). France (?), England (?), s. xiii. 235 x 158 mm. Parchment. Single leaf.

Double column; each column 153 x 47 mm.; 49 lines to a column; columns ruled in blue ink. Painted initial *P* (9-line) in blue, red, and pink on recto.

Provenance: 'De la libreria [illegible] N. 1' in lower margin on recto. Obtained by John Feldman from Ferrini, c. 1988/89 (details of provenance from Feldman, 1 November 1999). Gift of John Feldman, April 1991. (**BP**)

Pl. 1 **MS 325**: Latin Bible (part of Jerome's *Preface*). France, c. 1240. 173 x 60 mm. Parchment. Single leaf.

Single column; 153 x 50 mm.; 64 lines. Large historiated initial *F* on recto, gilded with green, gray, and reddish-brown coloring, depicting a seated man.

Provenance: Pencilled at bottom of recto 'France, c. 1240 005'; on verso in same position 'YTLLRZX'. Obtained by John Feldman from Ferrini, c. 1988/89 (details of provenance from Feldman, 1 November 1999). Donated by Feldman, April 1991. (**KS**)

MS 326: Latin Bible (part of Jerome's *Preface*). France, c. 1240. 218

x 139 mm. (cropped). Parchment. Single leaf.

Double column; each column 148 x 45 mm.; 55 lines to a column; ruled and bounded in drypoint. Large (8-line) illuminated and inhabited initial *F* on recto.

Provenance: Obtained by John Feldman from Ferrini, c. 1988/89 (details of provenance from Feldman, 1 November 1999). Donated by Feldman, April 1991. (**AS**)

MS 327: Psalter (?) (Psalms 89: 10 – 91: 14). France, s. xiii. 176 x 122 mm. Parchment. Single leaf.

Double column; each column 105 x 48 mm.; 30 lines to a column.

Provenance: Gift of Ellsworth Mason, 10 September 1985. (**BP**)

Pl. 14 **MS 328**: Latin Bible (Luke 17: 14 – 19: 36). Italy, second half of s. xiii. 288 x 202 mm. Parchment. Single leaf.

Double column; each column 175 x 54 mm.; 47 lines to a column.

Provenance: At bottom of verso in modern pencil '100–169–418 $50'.

MS 332: Unidentified series of *quaestiones* on the law of marriage. France, s. xiii / s. xiv. 208 x 137 mm. Parchment. Single leaf.

Double column; each column 150 x 48 mm.; 54 lines to a column. On verso, catchword elaborated to encompass a drawing of a two-headed creature, one head human, the other a mouse (?); marginal decoration in blue and gold extending down length of both inner margins of text.

Provenance: '4338O3R3a59Wo' in lower margin of recto. Purchased from Pirages, Catalogue 26, item 5, 14 June 1993 for $750.

Pl. 14 **MS 333 OS**: Augustine, *In Iohannis Evangelium tractatus CXXIV*: end of Homily 46 and beginning of Homily 47 (actually Homilies 45–46 in modern editions; cf. *Tractates on the Gospel of John 28–54*, ed. R. Willems, Corpus Christianorum, Series Latina, XXXVI

[1954], 397–98). Italy, probably Tuscany, mid s. xiii. 434 x 300 mm. Parchment. Single leaf.

Double column; each column 310 x 95 mm.; 44 lines to a column; ruled and bounded in drypoint; prick marks in inner margin.

Provenance: Purchased from Pirages, Catalogue 40, no. 1, on 17 November 1997. Other leaves from this MS:
- (i) one leaf, Quaritch, Catalogue 1036 (1984), no. 87;
- (ii) one leaf, Quaritch, Catalogue 1056 (1985), no. 83;
- (iii) one leaf, Quaritch, Catalogue 1147 (1991), no. 89 now in the Schøyen Collection, London and Oslo;
- (iv) one leaf, Sotheby's, 2 December 1997, lot 44 (formerly Neil F. Phillips MS 746);
- (v) two leaves, Sotheby's, 5 December 2000, lot 3;
- (vi) one leaf, Keio University, Tokyo, MS fragment 80202289.

It appears to have been circulating as separate leaves from 1966 when some were offered for sale by H. M. Fletcher (as noted in Sotheby's Catalogue, 2 December 1997). Purchased on the Walter Weir Fund. (**BP**)

MS 334 OS: Antiphonal (Matins for Passion Sunday). Italy, late s. xv. 551 x 400 mm. Parchment. Single leaf (framed).

Music: five 4-line staves in red with square notation and text for music in black ink. 370 x 272 mm.; ruled and bounded in plummet.

Provenance: Folio number '39' on top right recto; signature 'iii' on bottom right; no information on date of acquisition. (**DS**)

MS 338: Book of Hours (from the Hours of the Cross). Flanders (?), c. 1460. 170 x 124 mm. Parchment. Single leaf.

Single column; 112 x 71 mm.; 16 lines. Several foliate, gilded letters with red and blue ornamentation, and white tracery; rectangular line fillers half red, half blue ornamented with gold and white dots.

Provenance: Modern pencil '9' on top right corner of recto; on lower margin of verso '67601OB83FO115ST650'. Purchased from Pirages, Catalogue 40, no. 10, by UCB, May 1998 for $650. (**AS**)

MS 339: Memorandum in English and Latin recording payments to an estate in Shropshire, dated 29 September 1420. 205 x 120 mm. (maximum dimensions: the leaf is irregular). Parchment. Single leaf.

Provenance: Purchased from Pirages, May 1998 for $1,500 on the Walter Weir Fund. (**AS**)

MS 340: Indenture conveying two houses in Norfolk, 30 September 1453. 250 x 382 mm. Parchment. Single leaf.

Provenance: Purchased from Pirages, May 1998 for $350 on the Walter Weir Fund. (**PB**)

MS 341: Gregory the Great, *Homily* (*PL* 76, col. 969). Italy, s. xiii. 146 x 100 mm. Parchment. Single leaf.

Single column; 112 x 75 mm.; 24 lines.

Provenance: Purchased from Powell's Book Store, Chicago, May 1998 for $83 on the Walter Weir Fund. (**PB**)

MS 344: Horace, *Odes* (I. 19 – IV). Italy, s. xv. 217 x 132 mm. Paper. Ff. 55.

Single column; 130 x 80 mm.; 26 lines to the full column.

Collation: i, 1–5^{10}, 6^4. Originally part of a much larger work: the first surviving text leaf is numbered '120'.

Provenance: 'Parte Di / Orozio' (on title page); 'xxviijo ottobrij 1476 florencie' (rubricated colophon fol. 51r); bookplate of Richard Paget, 1786, 'Arthur Paget, 1859' on verso of flyleaf, 'XXII.5' below in pencil. Bound in green morocco gilt by Rivière. Acquired in 1998, from Quaritch; the gift of Eugene H. and Jane M. Wilson.

MS 345: Latin Bible (2 Peter 1: 20 – 1 John 2: 11). Paris, c. 1330. 294 x 200 mm. Parchment. Single leaf.

Double column; each column 187 x 57 mm.; 46 lines to a column; ruled and bounded in ink. Elaborate borders on both recto and verso, extending the length of all three vertical text margins and across width of lower columns, in blue, pink, and purple, with white tracery and painted and gilded foliage. On the recto, inner margin ascender elaborated into dragon. Several 2-line inhabited initials. Some top-lines ascenders elaborated into grotesque animal shapes.

Provenance: Came to the Abbey of St. Alban's in the mid-fourteenth century. Original MS sold Sotheby's, 6 July 1964; subsequently broken up. For details of the subsequent circulation of a number of leaves see Christopher de Hamel, 'A Leaf from a Bible Manuscript France, *circa* 1330', in *Fine Books and Book Collecting*, ed. Christopher de Hamel and Richard Linenthal (Leamington Spa, 1981), pp. 10–12 (with plate). Additional single leaves include:

(i)   Quaritch, Catalogue 1036 (1984), no. 76;
(ii)   Quaritch, Catalogue 1088 (1988), no. 74;
(iii)   Quaritch, Catalogue 1147 (1991), no. 22;
(iv)   Sotheby's, 1 June 1990, lot 47(4);
(v)   Sotheby's, 21 June 1994, lots 17–18;
(vi)   Maggs, Catalogue 1227 (1997), no. 33;
(vii)   Maggs, Catalogue 1249 (1998), no. 21;
(viii) a bifolium, Fogg, Catalogue 16 (1995), no. 62.

The present leaf formerly John Feldman MS 26; gift of Amy Vandersall, August 1998, in memory of Marie-Helene Richard Gantner.

MS 348: English private letter concerning manor of Whetlaw (=Whitlaw, Northumberland ?). France, late s. xiv / early s. xv. 183 x 298 mm. Paper. Single leaf (written only on one side).
Addressed to '[…] dame isabell / de Claxton dame horden.

Provenance: Co-purchased on Special Collections funds and the Walter Weir Fund in July 1998, from Quaritch.

MS 349: English indenture, 18 October 1489. 210 x 277 mm. Parchment. Single leaf.

Indenture between William Haghe and John Drouffeld concerning the marriage of Alice, daughter of the former, and Thomas, son of John Drouffeld.

Provenance: Co-purchased on Special Collections funds and the Walter Weir Fund in July 1998, from Quaritch.

MS 350: English indenture, 31 August 1468. 300 x 220 mm. Parchment. Single leaf.

Indenture concerning sale by John Horne to William Leuyngton (?) of 'londys and tenementys and rentis and seruyces'.

Provenance: *olim* Phillipps 30380; co-purchased on Special Collections funds and the Walter Weir Fund in July 1998, from Quaritch.

MS 351: Cloth merchant's account. Germany, second half of fifteenth century. 210 x 178 mm. Parchment. Bifolium.

Provenance: Co-purchased on Special Collections funds and the Walter Weir Fund in July 1998, from Quaritch.

MS 352: Notarial documents, dated 28 December 1437. Spain. 415 x 225 mm. (approximately). Parchment. Four bifolia.

Provenance: Purchased for $1,200 in June 1998, from Philadelphia Rare Books and Manuscript Co., PO Box 9536, Philadelphia, PA 19124, List 213, item 23.

MS 355: Gospel Book (Luke 11: 29–46). France or Germany, s. ix. 302 x 214 mm. Parchment. Single leaf.

Single column; 27 lines; unruled.

Provenance: From the collection of Mark Lansburgh; purchased Sotheby's, 22 June 1999, lot 17.

MS 356: Latin Bible (Mark 4: 18 – 7: 15). Paris, c. 1300. 144 x 96 mm. Parchment. Single leaf.

Double column; each column 144 x 96 mm.; 63 lines to a column; ruled and bounded. Red painted initial *F* (3-line) at beginning of chapter 5; other smaller red or blue painted capitals within text.

Provenance: Purchased in October 1999 from Philadelphia Rare Books and Manuscript Co.

Ege Collection

This portfolio, *Fifty Original Leaves from Medieval Manuscripts*, was purchased for $16,000 in honor of Professor Amy Vandersall, Professor of Fine Arts, in early 1989. Robert and Diane Greenlee contributed $15,000; the Friends of the Libraries donated $1,000 to the purchase. It was acquired from John Feldman who had obtained it from Ferrini.

This was one of a number of sets of portfolios produced by Otto Ege (1888–1951) during the course of a lengthy career of breaking up manuscripts (this one seems only to have circulated after his death). For some discussion of his life and activities see Christopher de Hamel, *Cutting up Manuscripts for Pleasure and Profit*, 1995 Sol Malkin Lecture in Bibliography (Charlottesville, 1996), especially pp. 16–18, and Roger Wieck, 'Folia Fugitiva: The Pursuit of the Illuminated Manuscript Leaf', *Journal of the Walters Art Gallery* 54 (1996): 233–53, especially pp. 248–49.

This is number 32 out of forty portfolios. Of the original fifty leaves it lacks those numbered 25, 30, 47, 48, 50. In addition, number 15 was not part of the original set; Ferrini had access to some of Ege's original labels and attached one to a new matt and added a different leaf in his possession (information from John Feldman, 8 August 2000).

Other sets of this portfolio are:
2.   Ohio State University
5.   Ohio University, Athens, Ohio
6.   University of Massachusetts, Amherst

9. Public Library of Cincinnati, Hamilton City, Ohio
12. Buffalo and Erie Public Library
13. University of Minnesota, Minneapolis
15. Kent State University
16. Art Gallery of Ontario, Toronto, Canada
19. State University of New York at Stonybrook
22. Cleveland Public Library, Ohio
24. Indiana University, Lilly Library
25. University of Saskatchewan, Saskatoon, Canada, Special Collections
27. University of South Carolina
28. Pierpont Morgan Library MS M. 1021
29. Lima Public Library, Ohio
30. Denison University
33. Christie's, 25 June 1997, lot 16 (sold to John Windle; now in a private collection in San Francisco)
35. Rochester Institute of Technology
37. Case Western Reserve University
38. University of North Carolina, Greensboro
39. Christie's, 30 January 1980, lot 212 (Maggs, £2,600)

We have not attempted to establish the degree of completeness of any of these portfolios, but it may be noted that no. 35 (Rochester Institute of Technology) has an extra leaf. It is conceivable that not all the portfolios were compiled from the same set of manuscripts or may have been subject to subsequent intermittent substitution or removal.

Ege's other portfolios include *Original Leaves from Famous Bibles: Nine Centuries 1121–1935 A.D.*, of which two series were issued, one of thirty-seven leaves, issued in 200 sets, one of sixty leaves, issued in 100 sets. This portfolio includes leaves from **Ege 6** below and possibly **Ege 5** and **Ege 9**. Copies, in part or whole, noted without differentiation of series or of state of completeness, are in Georgetown University, University of Iowa, University of Chicago, University of Kentucky, Michigan State University, Ohio State University, University of Tulsa, Bucknell University, Rhodes

College, Regis University, Beverly Hills Public Library, Claremont Colleges, Loyola Marymount University, Pepperdine University, UCLA, University of Redlands, Library of Congress, Concordia Theological Seminary, Earlham College, Berea College, Wellesley College, Princeton Theological School, Colgate University Divinity School, Saint Lawrence University, Public Library of Cincinnati, Bob Jones University, Amarillo Public Library, Dallas Public Library, Occidental College Library, University of California at Santa Cruz, Gleeson Library, University of San Francisco, Trinity College, Wellesley College, Bridwell Library, Southern Methodist University, Oberlin College, Lutheran Theological Seminary, Indiana University, New York State Library, Cleveland Public Library, Lima Public Library (Ohio), University of Houston, Denver Public Library, Samford University Library, Arizona State University, Bowling Green State University, Case Western Reserve University, Kent State University, Toledo-Lucas County Public Library, University of Pennsylvania, Center for Judaic Studies, Milwaukee County Federated Library System, Stanford University, Buffalo and Erie County Public Library, Colorado State University, Mayo Clinic.

Other leaves from **Ege 9** are included in another Ege portfolio, one of twenty-five leaves, *Original Leaves from Famous Books, Eight Centuries 1240 A.D.–1923 A.D.*, of which 110 sets were issued; copies have been located in Loyola Marymount University, University of California, San Diego Houghton Library, Harvard, Union College, New York, Cleveland Public Library, and Denver Public Library.

In addition, the portfolio *Original Leaves from Famous Books, Nine Centuries 1122 A.D.–1923 A.D.*, appears to contain further leaves from **Ege 40** as item 6. Fifty sets were issued, each of forty leaves; copies have been located in Colorado State University, Stanford University, University of California at Santa Cruz, Georgetown University, Mayo Clinic Library, Case Western Reserve University, Cleveland Public Library.

Leaves noted below under individual entries are in addition

to those in portfolios noted above.

Ege 1: Bible, New Testament (John 19: 7–19). Switzerland, early s. xii. 215 x 157 mm. Parchment.

Three columns: single central column of primary text (150 x 50 mm.); 18 lines to a column; ruled and bounded; with interlinear glosses in smaller form of same script. The inner and outer columns are of commentary, again in a smaller form of the same script. Divisions are marked here by paraff marks. On the verso another hand has inserted further commentary, mentioning Isidore's *Etymologies*; in the lower margin on the verso, a semi-cursive hand has added 11 lines (inc: ' … ones prima ut diabolum perligum uincetur').

Provenance: Numbered '84' in ink in upper right outer margin; also numbered '8' in pencil in upper right outer margin. Possibly Sotheby's, 26 November 1985, lot 43 (18 leaves). Single leaf in UCLA 2/XII/GER/2; two leaves, collection of Dr. Christopher de Hamel, London; possibly other leaves in Ege's portfolio, *Original Leaves from Bibles*. (**AV**)

Ege 2: Missal. Spain, second half s. xii. 335 x 235 mm. Parchment.

Single column; 250 x 170 mm.; 24 lines. Frequent rubricated headings; red painted initials (2-, 4-, 6-, 7-line) some with flourishing.

Provenance: MS originally owned by Arnold Mettler of St. Gall; his sale, Parke-Bernet, 30 November 1948, lot 317 (173 leaves); subsequently broken up:

(i)   one leaf, Maggs, Bulletin 11 (1982), no. 23 (plate 5);

(ii)   four leaves, Sotheby's, 25 April 1983, lot 16;

(iii)   one leaf, Sotheby's, 25 June 1985, lot 7(i);

(iv)   twenty-six leaves, Sotheby's, 26 November 1985, lot 44 to Maggs;

(v)   one leaf, Sotheby's, 2 December 1997, lot 45; from the collection of Neil Phillips (MS 1117);

(vi)   one leaf, Dunedin, New Zealand, Reed Fragment 51; described in Margaret Manion, et al., *Medieval and Renaissance Manuscripts in New Zealand Collections* (London, 1989), p. 108, no. 113; from Quaritch, Catalogue 1056 (1985), no. 63;

(vii)   one leaf, Quaritch, Catalogue 1036 (1984), no. 8;

(viii)   three leaves, Christie's, 9 July 2001, lot 2;

(ix)   two leaves, collection of Dr. Barbara Shailor;

(x)   one leaf, Maggs, *Illuminations*, Catalogue 1319 (2001), no. 65.

Ege 3: Lectionary (John 1: 27–28, Luke 1: 26–42). Italy, mid. s. xii. 320 x 236 mm. Parchment.

Single column; 230 x 130 mm.; 22 lines; ruled and bounded. Some painted red initials (one 7-line, one 4-line) with blue and red flourishing; rubricated headings.

Provenance: '126' in upper right recto corner in modern hand;

(i)   one leaf, Maggs, Catalogue 1227 (1997), no. 76;

(ii)   one leaf, Pirages, Catalogue 46 (2001), no. 1021;

(iii)   possibly one leaf, Colorado College, Tutt Library, Donald Jackson Collection no. 1. (**RF**)

Ege 4: Psalter. France, late s. xii. 210 x 155 mm. Parchment.

Single column; 158 x 90 mm.; 33 lines; ruled and bounded.

Some subject headings (e.g., 'subiectio', 'humilitas', 'bellum') added in outer margins. (**BGH**)

Ege 5: Bible (Genesis 37: 5 – 41: 7). France, early s. xiii. 310 x 215 mm. Parchment.

Double column; each column 200 x 53 mm.; 60 lines to a column; ruled and bounded. Several 2-line initials, alternately red and blue; running title ('GE' / 'XXXVIII') alternate letters/numbers in red and blue.

Provenance: '2 [cropped]' in ink in bottom left recto corner. Possibly two leaves, Columbia University Med/Ren Frag 22–23. (**AV**)

Pl. 8 **Ege 6**: Latin Bible. England (Cambridge?), early s. xiii. 275 x 202 mm. Parchment.

Double column; each column 193 x 47 mm.; 60 lines to a column; ruled and bounded; prick marks visible. Running title with alternate letters/numbers in red and blue.

Provenance: '89' in upper outer margin in pencil. Complete Bible sold Sotheby's, 21 December 1948, lot 421 (to Maggs), and broken up:

(i)   two leaves, Boston University, STh MS Leaves 36–37 (Oliver, no. 17);

(ii)   three leaves, Boston, Endowment for Biblical Research, MS Leaves 16–18 (Oliver, no. 16);

(iii)   123 leaves, Sotheby's, 26 November 1985, lot 49;

(iv)   six leaves, Sotheby's, 25 April 1983, lot 18;

(v)   one leaf, Sotheby's, 21 June 1994, lot 8(a);

(vi)   one leaf, Maggs, European Bulletin 17 (1992), no. 25;

(vii)   one leaf, Maggs, European Bulletin 21 (1997), no. 3;

(viii) one leaf, Maggs, *Illuminations*, Catalogue 1319 (2001), no. 66;

(ix)   other leaves in *Original Leaves from Medieval Manuscripts offered for sale by the Staff Loan Fund Association, Lima Public Library* (Lima, Ohio).

Pl. 12 **Ege 7**: Petrus Riga, *Aurora*. England, early s. xiii. 235 x 113 mm. Parchment.

Single column; 190 x 70 mm.; 47 lines; ruled and bounded. 5-line colored initials, blue with red penwork, red with blue.

Provenance:

(i)   one leaf, Quaritch, Catalogue 1036 (1984), no. 125;

(ii)   one leaf, Quaritch, Catalogue 1270 (2000), no. 113;

(iii)   twelve leaves, Schøyen collection (London and Oslo), MS 1643;

(iv)   twenty-nine leaves, Sotheby's, 26 November 1985, lot 48;

(v)   three leaves, Boston, Endowment for Biblical Research

MS Leaves 8–10 (Oliver, no. 18);

(vi)   one leaf, Boston University, STh MS Leaf 17 (Oliver, no. 19);

(vii)   other leaves in *Original Leaves from Medieval Manuscripts offered for sale by the Staff Loan Fund Association, Lima Public Library* (Lima, Ohio). (**BGH**)

Ege 8: Gradual. England, s. xiii. 181 x 120 mm. Parchment.
Single column; ruled in 4-line noted staves; 132 x 81 mm.
Provenance: two leaves, Sotheby's, 20 June 1995, lot 6(i). (**KM**)

Ege 9: Bible (2 Kings 8: 17 – 12: 13). France (Paris), mid. s. xiii. 170 x 120 mm. Parchment.

Double column; each column 112 x 37 mm.; 53 lines to a column; ruled and bounded. 2- or 4-line colored initials, red with blue penwork, blue with red.

Provenance: One leaf Boston University, MS Leaf 90, Hawley Collection (Oliver, no. 30); other leaves included in another Ege portfolio *Original Leaves from Famous Books, Eight Centuries 1240 A.D.–1923 A.D.* (**BGH**)

Ege 10: Psalter (Psalms 112: 7 – 113: 9). Germany, mid. s. xiii. 195 x 140 mm. Parchment.

Single column; 135 x 92 mm.; 20 lines; ruled and bounded. Bar border running full length of text and into lower margin, in blue and gold with white tracery on recto; frequent 1-line initials either in gold with blue penwork or blue with red penwork; line fillers in various styles.

Provenance:

(i)   three leaves, Sotheby's, 26 November 1985, lot 51;

(ii)   one leaf, Maggs, *Illuminations*, Catalogue 1319 (2001), no. 68. (**BP**)

Ege 11: Bible (Judith 7: 11 – 10: 2). Italy, mid. s. xiii. 197 x 130 mm. Parchment.

Double column; each column 128 x 38 mm.; 50 lines to a column; ruled and bounded in plummet. Blue painted initials with red penwork (6-, 8-line). (**KS**)

Ege 12: Psalter (Psalms 65: 10–20, 66: 1–8, 67: 1–3). France, mid. s. xiii. 135 x 100 mm. Parchment.

Single column; 100 x 65 mm.; 22 lines; ruled and bounded. Some 3-line gilt initials on a purple and red ground with white tracery; numerous 1-line initials generally alternating blue and gilt.

Provenance: Probably from MS in *Census*, II, p. 1939, no. 13; one leaf, Sotheby's, 1 December 1998, lot 15(a). (**BGH**)

Pl. 10 **Ege 13**: Bible (Ecclesiastes 31: 19 – 35: 17). England (Oxford?), mid. s. xiii. 195 x 139 mm. Parchment.

Double column; each column 137 x 45 mm.; 48 lines to a column; ruled and bounded. Several 2-line illuminated initials, either in blue on a purple ground, or purple on a blue ground, both with white tracery; 3-line painted initials, blue with red penwork or red with blue.

Provenance:
(i)   ten leaves, Sotheby's, 25 April 1983, lot 25, to Lubin;
(ii)   one leaf, Boston, Endowment for Biblical Research MS Leaf 14 (Oliver, no. 20);
(iii) one leaf, Maggs, *Illuminations*, Catalogue 1319 (2001), no. 69. (**BP**)

Pl. 12 **Ege 14**: Bible (Ezechiel 33: 1 – 35: 3). France, late s. xiii. 404 x 267 mm. Parchment.

Double column; each column 282 x 85 mm.; 50 lines to a column; ruled and bounded. Foliate bar borders in inner margins of inner column on recto and both columns on verso, the latter with gold studding.

Provenance: Original MS sold Parke-Bernet, 30 November 1948, lot 326, 503 leaves, and subsequently broken up:

(i)   one leaf, Sotheby's, New York, 9 April 1980, lot 227;

(ii)   one leaf, the Rendells, Catalogue 146 (1979), no. 67;

(iii)   one leaf, Sotheby's, 25 April 1983, lot 834;

(iv)   210 leaves, Sotheby's, 11 December 1984, lot 39;

(v)   four leaves, Sotheby's, 23 June 1993, lot 19;

(vi)   two leaves, Sotheby's, 21 June 1994, lot 109;

(vii)   one leaf, Sotheby's, 1 December 1998, lot 12;

(viii) three leaves, acquired by Metropolitan Museum of Art in 1998, the gift of William D. Wixon; see William D. Wixon, ed., *Mirror of the Medieval World* (New York, 1999), no. 141, pp. 118–19.

(ix)   one leaf, Endowment for Biblical Research, MS Leaf 73 (Oliver, no. 35);

(x)   one leaf, Boston University STh MS Leaf 38 (Oliver, no. 36);

(xi)   one leaf, Rutgers University Library. (**AV**)

Pl. 13 **Ege 15**: Missal. France (?), late s. xiii. 287 x 196 mm. Parchment.

Double column; each column 200 x 60/70 mm.; 15 lines to a column; ruled and bounded. 3-line illuminated initial *S* in blue, with orange, pink, white, and green pigments, with gold studding and tracery (on both recto and verso); 3-line initial *U* in gilt, blue, pink, and white (verso); rubricated passages in lower (recto) and inner (verso) margins; painted line fillers in blue and purple with white penwork within a gilded frame.

Provenance: Originally from the collection of Henri Auguste Brölemann, sold by his great-grand-daughter at Sotheby's, 5 May 1926, lot 161, and subsequently broken up; other leaves:

(i)   one leaf, Sotheby's, 26 November 1985, lot 61;

(ii)   one leaf, Sotheby's, 5 December 1994, lot 4;

(iii)   one leaf, Quaritch, Catalogue 1147 (1991), no. 60;

(iv)   one leaf, Quaritch, Catalogue 1270 (2000), no. 79;

(v)   one leaf, Maggs, Bulletin 11 (1982), no. 43;

(vi)   one leaf, Cleveland Museum of Art, acc. 82.141;

(vii)   one leaf, Boston Public Library MS 1538;

(viii)   one leaf, Houghton pf. MS Typ. 405;
(ix)   one leaf, Boston, Endowment for Biblical Research, MS Leaf 86 (Oliver, no. 63);
(x)   one leaf, now owned by Dr. Mario Volente, 346 North Bowling Green Way, Los Angeles, CA 90049;
(xi)   one leaf, Beinecke Library, MS 712;
(xii)   one leaf, Beinecke Library, MS 804;
(xiii)   one leaf, Sotheby's, 19 June 2001, lot 9;
(xiv)   one leaf, Metropolitan Museum 1992.238;
(xv)   one leaf, collection of Dr. Christopher de Hamel, London;
(xvi)   two leaves, Ferrini, Catalogue 1 (1987), nos. 48–49 (with plate).

Oliver (no. 63) adds leaves in Hollins College (no. 11), Buffalo and Erie Public Library; Sibley Music Library, Eastman School of Music Rochester; Glencairn Museum, Bryn Athyn, Pennsylvania. (**PB**)

Note: In the Colorado portfolio this leaf not from the original portfolio, but provided by Ferrini.

Ege 16: Breviary. France, late s. xiii. 103 x 70 mm. Parchment.

Single column; 60 x 41 mm.; 21 lines; ruled and bounded. 1- and 2-line gilt initials on blue and red ground, with white tracery and gold studding. Frequent rubrication.

Provenance: Possibly six leaves, Sotheby's, 26 November 1985, part of lot 74; '235', in a modern hand, in pencil, in the top outer recto margin. (**BGH**)

Ege 17: Psalter. England, late s. xiii. 170 x 115 mm. Parchment.

Double column; each column 120 x 35/40 mm.; 20 lines to a column; ruled and bounded. Floral border runs the length of the inner, verso margin. Frequent 3-line gilt initials, infilled in either blue or purple on a blue or purple ground, some with tracery and gold studding. One 6-line and one 4-line in gold, blue, and purple; decorated line fillers in blue or purple and gold.

Provenance: one leaf, Sotheby's, 21 June 1994, lot 12(c). (**PB**)

Ege 18: Breviary. France, late s. xiii. 148 x 110 mm. (cropped). Parchment.

Double column; each column 114 x 37 mm.; 28 lines to a column; ruled and bounded. Several 2-line painted initials either blue with red penwork or red with blue.

Provenance: ninety leaves, Sotheby's, 26 November 1985, lot 59. (**BGH**)

Ege 19: Bible (Joel 3: 3–21, Amos 1: 1 – 3: 5). Italy, early s. xiv. 171 x 234 mm. Parchment.

Double column; each column 154 x 48 mm.; 48 lines to a column; ruled and bounded in ink. 8-line illuminated initial marking beginning of Amos; other smaller painted initials either red with blue penwork or blue with red.

Provenance:
(i)   one leaf, Quaritch, Catalogue 1056 (1985), no. 20;
(ii) eighteen leaves, Sotheby's, 26 November 1985, lot 60. (**BGH**)

Ege 20: Psalter (Psalms 40: 7 – 41: 4). Netherlands, early s. xiv. 125 x 92 mm. Parchment.

Single column; 69 x 47 mm.; 16 lines; ruled and bounded. Illuminated and painted initials.

Provenance: eighteen leaves, Sotheby's, 26 November 1985, lot 58. (**KS**)

Ege 21: Hymnal. France, early s. xiv. 163 x 110 mm. Parchment.

Single column; 100 x 60 mm.; ruled in red in staves, 7 staves to a column. Pendant spear border, in blue and pink; one illuminated 5-line initial *S* with floral decoration; illuminated line filler. (**AV**)

Ege 22: Noted Missal (John 21: 3–14, Acts 8: 26–32). Germany

(Wartburg), early s. xiv. 360 x 260 mm. Parchment.

Double column; each column 289 x 88 mm.; 31 lines to a column; ruled and bounded in ink. Painted initials of various sizes, either blue or red; rubricated headings; initial letter of each line touched in red.

Provenance: *olim* Phillipps 516; sold Sotheby's, 1 December 1947, lot 92, 232 leaves:

(i)   The bulk of this MS now seems to be Toronto, Bergendal MS 69, comprising 125 leaves; sold Sotheby's, 11 December 1984, lot 52; see Joseph Pope, *One Hundred and Twenty Five Manuscripts: Bergendal Collection Catalogue* (Toronto, 1999);

(ii)   nineteen leaves, Sotheby's, 26 November 1985, lot 62;

(iii)   two leaves, Boston, Endowment for Biblical Research MS Leaves 77–78 (Oliver, no. 68). (**BGH**)

Ege 23: Breviary. France, mid s. xiv. 176 x 117 mm. Parchment.

Double column; each column 142 x 36 mm.; 32 lines to a column; ruled and bounded. Initials of various sizes in blue with red penwork; rubricated headings; some underlining in red. (**BGH**)

Ege 24: Book of Hours. England, mid. s. xiv. 173 x 125 mm. Parchment.

Double column; each column 114 x 31 mm.; 30 lines to a column; ruled and bounded in ink. Penwork initials, either pink or blue on gilded ground; foliate decoration in upper and lower inner margins on both recto and verso; rubricated headings. (**BGH**)

Ege 25: *not present.*

Ege 26: Missal. France (Rouen), late s. xiv. 292 x 213 mm. Parchment.

Double column; each column 292 x 213 mm.; 31 lines to a column; ruled and bounded in plummet. 1-, 2-line gilded initials on blue, red, and gilt ground with white flourishes; some rubrication and underlining in red; some letters touched in yellow.

Provenance: four leaves, Sotheby's, 26 November 1985, part of lot 63, and again 20 June 1995, part of lot 7. (**DS**)

Ege 27: Antiphonal. Italy, early s. xv. 398 x 288 mm. Parchment.

Single column; ruled in red ink in seven 4-line staves. Painted 4- and 7-line initials, blue with red penwork, red with blue. Some initials infilled in yellow. (**BGH**)

Ege 28: Book of Hours. France, mid. s. xv. 150 x 116 mm. Parchment.

Single column; 87 x 61 mm., 15 lines; ruled in plummet. Frequent 1-, 3-line gilded initials on blue and purple grounds; frequent blue and purple line fillers. Ruled vertical border in two columns of gilt and blue respectively, divided by white rule; gilt tracery extending into upper and lower margins. (**KM**)

Ege 29: Book of Hours (Psalm 5: 2–9). France, mid. s. xv. 186 x 134 mm. Parchment.

Single column; 90 x 60 mm.; 14 lines; ruled and bounded in purplish ink. Frequent 1-line (and occasional 2-line) gilded initials, infilled in blue on a purple ground.

Provenance: twelve leaves, Sotheby's, 26 November 1985, part of lot 74. (**BGH**)

Ege 30: *not present.*

Ege 31: Book of Hours. France, mid. s. xv. 186 x 130 mm. Parchment.

Single column; 105 x 63 mm.; 15 lines. Foliate borders in outer recto and verso margins, with blue thistle, red berries, and white flowers. Numerous 1-line (and one 2-line) gilded initials with white scrollwork, on blue and mauve grounds; line fillers in blue, mauve, and gold; rubricated headings.

Provenance: Measurements are identical to a leaf, with miniature, from a Parisian Book of Hours, sold Sotheby's, 26 November 1985, lot 67 and again Sotheby's, 20 June 1997, lot 14; two leaves, Boston, Endowment for Biblical Research, MS Leaves 27–28 (Oliver, no. 98). (**AV**)

Ege 32: Psalter and Breviary. Italy, mid. s. xv. 264 x 208 mm. Parchment.

Single column; 172 x 123 mm.; 20 lines; ruled and bounded. One 3-line gold initial with purple penwork, one 2-line blue painted initial with red penwork; rubricated headings; blue paraffs.

Provenance: Originally bought by Ege in Florence in 1928 (*Census*, II, p. 1942, no. 38); sixty-one leaves, Sotheby's, 26 November 1985, lot 68.

Ege 33: Missal. Germany, mid. s. xv. 370 x 275 mm. Parchment.

Double column; each column 247 x 80 mm.; 35 lines to a column; ruled and bounded in brown ink. Two large (one 6-line, the other 7-line) blue painted initials; two 2-line painted initials, one blue, one red; various blue or red 1-line initials; some initials touched with red vertical stroke.

Provenance: seventeen leaves, Sotheby's, 25 November 1985, lot 69. (**DS**)

Ege 34: Noted Psalter. Italy, mid s. xv. 387 x 284 mm. Parchment.

Single column; 276 x 197 mm.; 22 lines. Beginning of each verse marked by 1-line painted initials, alternately blue and red; one 2-line initial with purple penwork; frequent rubrication.

Provenance: '20' in upper, outer recto margin. (**AS**)

Ege 35: St. Jerome, *Contra Jovinianum*. France, mid. s. xv. 387 x 280 mm. Parchment.

Double column; each column 255 x 75 mm.; 41 lines to a column. Two 1-line gilt initials; several 1-line painted initials;

frequent rubrication; first letter of each sentence touched in red.

Provenance:

(i)   four leaves, Sotheby's, 26 November 1985, part of lot 81;

(ii) one leaf, Sotheby's, 20 June 1995, lot 6(4). (**BGH**)

Ege 36: Book of Hours. France, mid. s. xv. 107 x 66 mm. Parchment.

Single column; 49 x 32 mm.; 13 lines; ruled and bounded in red. Some 2-line gilt initials, infilled in blue, purple, and white; rectangular line filler in blue, purple, and white.

Provenance: 14 leaves, Sotheby's, 26 November 1985, part of lot 74. (**KS**)

Ege 37: Epistolary (Ephesians 4: 23–28, 5: 15–21, 6: 10–13). Italy, mid. s. xv. 290 x 212 mm. Parchment.

Single column; 210 x 140 mm.; 21 lines. Frequent rubricated initials of various sizes.

Provenance: one leaf, University of Utah, Rare Books MS lat. frag. 7. (**AS**)

Ege 38: Missal. France (Limoges), mid. s. xv. 310 x 240 mm. Parchment.

Double column; each column 210 x 70 mm.; 29 lines to a column; ruled and bounded. 2-line initials, blue with red penwork or red with blue penwork; some 1-line blue initials; headings and some proper names rubricated.

Provenance: Possibly originally Hodgson's, 30 April 1914, lot 510; subsequently broken up:

(i)   twelve leaves, Sotheby's, 26 November 1985, lot 73;

(ii) one leaf, Sotheby's, 21 June 1994, lot 8(c). (**PB**)

Pl. 11 **Ege 39**: Livy, *History of Rome*. Italy, mid. s. xv. 223 x 155 mm. Parchment.

Single column; 110 x 161 mm.; 24 lines.

Provenance: Originally sold Sotheby's, 23 January 1950, lot

461; partly resold, Sotheby's, 11 December 1984, lot 51 (this part now Bodleian Library, Lat. class. e. 52, to which has been added one leaf donated by University of North Carolina, Greensboro, from their portfolio no. 38; see Peter Kidd, *Bodleian Library Record* 16 [1998]: 272–73); in addition:

- (i) one leaf, Durham University Library, Archives and Special Collections, fragments portfolio II, no. 29 (purchased from Maggs, 1980);
- (ii) one leaf, Sotheby's, 26 November 1985, lot 81; now part of Bodleian Library Lat. class. e. 52. fol. 131;
- (iii) one leaf, Quaritch, Catalogue 1036 (1984), no. 5 (with plate); now part of Bodleian Library Lat. class. e. 52. fol. 128;
- (iv) one leaf, private collection of Marcia Colish;
- (v) Boston University STh MS Leaf 83;
- (vi) one leaf, collection of Dr. Christopher de Hamel, London.

Copied by the Florentine scribe Giacomo Curlo; on his activities and the breaking up of this manuscript, see A. C. de la Mare, 'A Livy Copied by Giacomo Curlo Dismembered by Otto Ege', in *Interpreting and Collecting Fragments of Medieval Books*, ed. Linda L. Brownrigg and Margaret M. Smith (Los Altos Hills, Calif., 2000), pp. 57–88; we owe our knowledge of (vi) above to this article. (**RF**)

Ege 40: Thomas Aquinas, *Commentary on the Sentences*. Italy, late s. xv. 285 x 210 mm. Parchment.

Double column; each column 177 x 55/60 mm.; 37 lines to a column; ruled and bounded. One 3-line blue penwork initial; paraff signs alternately blue and red.

Provenance: Originally 309 leaves:

- (i) thirty-two leaves, Sotheby's, 26 November 1985, lot 80 with references to other leaves;
- (ii) one leaf ('260'), University of Utah, Rare Books MS Lat. frag. 9;

(iii)   one leaf, Maggs, Catalogue 1227 (1997), no. 96;
(iv)   one leaf, collection of Dr. Christopher de Hamel, London. (**BGH**)

Ege 41: Gregory the Great, *Dialogues*. France, late s. xv. 305 x 225 mm. Parchment.

Double column; each column 200 x 67 mm.; 40 lines to a column; ruled. One 2-line blue initial *F* with red penwork; several simple blue and red 1-line initials.

Provenance: Originally ff. 274 (see *Census*, II, 1945, no. 56); purchased by Ege from Thorpe (Guildford), c. 1925 and broken up:
(i)   thirty-three leaves, Sotheby's, 26 November 1985, lot 70;
(ii)   one leaf, Maggs, Bulletin 11 (1982), no. 88;
(iii)   one leaf, Maggs, Bulletin 21 (1997), no. 66;
(iv)   one leaf, collection of Dr. Christopher de Hamel, London;
(v)   one leaf, Maggs, *Illuminations*, Catalogue 1319 (2001), no. 111;
(vi)   other leaves in *Original Leaves from Medieval Manuscripts offered for sale by the Staff Loan Fund Association, Lima Public Library* (Lima, Ohio). (**TN**)

Ege 42: Psalter (Psalms 11: 4 – 14: 1). Germany (Würzburg), late s. xv. 440 x 300 mm. Parchment.

Single column; 302 x 245 mm.; 23 lines; ruled and bounded in ink. 1- or 2-line painted initials in blue or red. Rubrication; musical notation on recto. (**KS**)

Ege 43: Book of Hours. Netherlands, late s. xv. 168 x 129 mm. Parchment.

Single column; 105 x 75 mm.; 18 lines. Frequent 1-line painted initials in blue or red; occasional larger painted blue or red initials; some rubrication. (**RF**)

Ege 44: Bible (Ezra 8: 34 – 10: 11). Germany, late s. xv. 415 x 278 mm. Parchment.

Double column; each column 305 x 90 mm.; 34 lines to a column; bounded. Some painted 3-line initials in blue or red; some rubrication; initial letter of each verse touched in red.

Provenance:
(i)   one leaf, Boston University MS Leaf 81, Endowment Collection;
(ii)   nine leaves, Endowment for Biblical Research STh MS Leaves 8–16;
(iii)   other leaves included in another Ege portfolio *Original Leaves from Famous Books, Eight Centuries 1240 A.D.–1923 A.D.* (**BGH**)

Ege 45: Book of Hours. France, late s. xv. 188 x 134 mm. Parchment.

Single column; 90 x 63 mm.; 12 lines; ruled and bounded in red ink. 1- or 2-line illuminated initials, on rose, blue, white, and gilt ground, with line fillers in same style. (**DS**)

Ege 46: Book of Hours. Northern France, late s. xv. 162 x 121 mm. Parchment.

Single column; 95 x 68 mm.; 16 lines; ruled and bounded in red ink.

Foliate borders on both recto and verso, with red/purple buds, red flowers and gold and red buds, with green leaves, with gold studding; occasional 2-line illuminated initials.

Provenance: One leaf, Maggs, *Illuminations*, Catalogue 1319 (2001), no. 95. (**DS**)

Ege 47: *not present.*

Ege 48: *not present.*

Ege 49: Missal. Germany, early s. xvi. 395 x 265 mm. Parchment (stub of conjugate leaf attached).

Double column; each column 283 x 95 mm.; 35 lines to a column; bounded in red ink and ruled in brown crayon. Several 3-line painted initials in blue or red and some 1-line initials of the same kind; headings and names of authorities rubricated. (**AV**)

Provenance: one leaf, Boston, Endowment for Biblical Research MS Leaf 82 (Oliver, no. 69); one leaf, Boston University STh MS Leaf 54 (Oliver, no. 70).

Ege 50: *not present*.

James Hayes Collection
of Manuscripts and Printed Leaves

James Hayes (1907–93) was a calligrapher who was educated and worked in Chicago for more than fifty years. In 1972 he moved to Colorado. For an appreciation of Hayes's life and work see *The Colorado Calligraphers' Guild Newsletter* 16.2 (June 1996): 1–11.

Hayes's collection had been assembled over a number of years and included, in addition to medieval manuscript leaves, both early printing and post-medieval materials. It was purchased by UCB in 1994. The Colorado Calligraphers' Guild was instrumental in its acquisition.

Pl. 7   **Hayes 1**: Psalter. Italy, c. 1485. 117 x 78 mm. Parchment bifolium. Single column; 70 x 45 mm.; ruled.

Written by Bartolomeo Sanvito, on whom see A.C. de la Mare, 'The Florentine Scribes of Cardinal Giovanni of Aragon', *Il Libro e Il Testo, Atti del Convegno Internazionale*, ed. C. Questa and R. Raffaelli (Urbino, 1984), pp. 245–93, especially Appendix III. A, 'Manuscripts copied by Barolomeo Sanvito' (pp. 285–88), which lists twenty-one manuscripts written by him, and Appendix III. B, 'Manuscripts written by other scribes but rubricated by Sanvito' (pp. 288–89), which lists a further eleven manuscripts; neither list includes the Hayes leaves.

Provenance: Given to Hayes by Ege on 14 April 1949 (according to letter in accompanying file). Other leaves:

    (i)   one leaf, Sotheby's, 26 November 1985, lot 83 (with

plate), now in collection of Scott Dickerson, 355a Judah St., San Francisco, CA 94122;

(ii)   one leaf, Swann Galleries, 25 September 1980, lot 220, now in private hands in London;

(iii)   one leaf, Oberlin College;

(iv)   eight leaves, Boston University STh MS Leaves 72–80.

Hayes 2: Music MSS. St. Gall, s. xii. Parchment. Three separate fragments:

(i)–(ii) 200 x 137/38 mm; single column; ruled in red. Frequent 1- and 2-line red painted initials; rubricated response signs; musical notation; both leaves faded and stained.

(iii) 300 x 75 mm.; musical notation on verso (?), of different kind from (i)–(ii); faded and stained. This appears to be from a different MS from (i)–(ii).

See further Martin Picker, 'A Twelfth-Century Musical Manuscript in the Rutgers University Libraries,' *Journal of the Rutgers University Libraries* 52 (1990): 1–6.

Hayes 3: Book of Hours (Office of the Dead), Netherlands (?), second half of s. xv. 168 x 114 mm. Parchment. Single leaf.

Single column; 113 x 70 mm.; 24 lines. Ruled rectangular borders on both recto and verso, with flowers and tracery in red, orange, blue, green, and gray; one 2-line initial, in blue and white on a gilt ground; each verse marked by 1-line gilt initials on (alternately) blue or red with gilt designs; line fillers alternately blue or red with gilt designs; rubricated headings.

Hayes 4: Bible. France (?), early s. xiv (?). 158 x 105/10 mm. Parchment. Three bifolia: [1] Psalms 43: 2–10, 44: 3–12; [2] Psalms 56: 3–12, 61: 2–10; [3] Isaiah 12: 4–6, 38: 10-14.

Single column; 90 x 63 mm.; 15 lines; ruled. Several elaborate 2-line historiated initials: *N* on pink and blue ground, incorporating a winged dragon on a gold ground, with black flourishing, extending into upper and lower margins; *D* incorporating a serpent on a gilt background, with flourishing extending along upper margin; *E* divided into two parts by medial stroke: upper lobe contains zoomorphic grotesque with pink head, blue body, and red tail; lower lobe contains four-legged creature with a bird head; both parts are on a blue ground; 1-line gilded initials with blue penwork; painted blue initials with red penwork various forms of line filler, many gilded.

Hayes 5: Book of Hours (?). France (?), 1450. 171 x 127 mm. Parchment. Single leaf.

Single column; 95 x 65 mm.; 16 lines; ruled and bounded. Rectangular borders on recto and verso, 98 x 22 mm., with green leaves, blue acanthus leaves, and red strawberries, with other shades of mauve, the outer margin of which is ruled in blue, the inner in purple and gilt. 1-line gilt initials, infilled and/or on purple and blue grounds, with white tracery; rectangular line fillers, in purple and blue, with white tracery and gold studding.

Hayes 6: Book of Hours (?), France (?) / Flanders (?), s. xv. 170 x 118 mm. Parchment. Single leaf.

Single column; 99 x 62 mm.; 21 lines; ruled and bounded in black ink. Rectangular borders, recto and verso, 100 x 20 mm., ruled in black ink, both incorporating a bird in pink and gray and flowers in red, green, blue, and gray. 2-line gray white initials, both set within a square frame, decorated in red and blue, both with marginal flourishing in blue, gold, and red; rubricated headings and responses.

Hayes 7: Book of Hours. France, c. 1420. 238 x 191 mm. Parchment. Five leaves: 2 bifolia, 1 single leaf (from Calendar).

Single column; 102 x 70 mm.; 15 lines for text, 19 for Calendar. Several demi-vinets with flowers in blue and pink with frequent gold studding.

Pl. 9 **Hayes 8**: Book of Hours. Italy, s. xv. 145 x 95 mm. Parchment. Five leaves: 2 bifolia, 1 single leaf.

Single column; 88 x 55 mm.; 15 lines.

Provenance: possibly from a fragmentary Book of Hours in Otto Ege collection (*Census* II, p. 1945, no. 55); written by Pietro Ursuleo.

Pl. 6 **Hayes 9**: Terence, Plays. Italy (probably Florence), s. xv. 250 x 175 mm. Parchment. Five leaves: 2 bifolia, 1 single leaf.

Single column; 165 x 110 mm.; 30 lines; ruled in drypoint. Blue, 4-line painted initials; names of performers in pale red capitals, some in margin.

Written by the Florentine humanist scribe Julianus Antonii de Prato; see A.C. de la Mare, 'A Livy Copied by Giacomo Curlo Dismembered by Otto Ege', in *Interpreting and Collecting Fragments of Medieval Books*, ed. Linda L. Brownrigg and Margaret M. Smith (Los Altos Hills, Calif., 2000), p. 57, note (1c) and previously ascribed by her to 'Messer Marco' in 'New Research on Humanistic Scribes in Florence,' *Miniatura fiorentina del Rinascimento 1440–1525. Un primo Censura*, 2 vols., ed. A. Garzelli (Florence, 1985), I, pp. 395–475, especially 512–13, 597.

Provenance: From a MS sold Sotheby's, 28 May 1934, lot 100 (then 103 leaves); bought by Dawson's of Los Angeles and sold to Otto Ege who broke it up (see *Census*, II, p. 1947, no. 65):

- (i) seven leaves, Sotheby's, 26 November 1985, lot 78; one of these resold Sotheby's, 2 December 1997, lot 66 (collection of Neil Phillips); others (ii) and (iii) below;
- (ii) one leaf, Quaritch, Catalogue 1088 (1988), no. 90;
- (iii) one leaf, Quaritch, Catalogue 1147 (1991), no. 117;
- (iv) one leaf, Quaritch, Catalogue 1270 (2000), no. 124;
- (v) one leaf, Pirages, Catalogue 41 [n.d., c. 1997], no. 60;
- (vi) one leaf, Maggs, Bulletin 12 (1984), item 64;
- (vii) one leaf, Maggs, Bulletin 22 (1998), no. 82 (with plate);
- (viii) two leaves, Boston University STh MS Leaves 81–82 (Oliver, no. 117);

(ix)   one leaf, Vassar College Library Grille Folio 091 Sp. 3
       (12);
(x)   one leaf, Sweet Briar College;
(xi)   one leaf, Rutgers University Library;
(xii) one leaf, Columbia University Med/Ren Frag 04.

Hayes 10: Gregory, *Moralia in Job* (XXIV: viii, 20 – x, 24). Italy (?),
s. xi. 242 x 277 mm. Parchment (cropped); probably binder's
waste.

Double column; each column 216 x 115 mm.; 28 lines to a
column.

Provenance: Given to Hayes in December 1965, by the Caxton
Club of Chicago, in 'appreciation for the many years of fruitful
and generous contribution of his talents'. (**BGH**)

Hayes 11: Martyrum (?). Salzburg (?), s xii. 305 x 222 mm. Parchment. Single leaf.

Single column; 235 x 150 mm.; 29 lines; bounded but not
ruled, but prick marks visible. Some red painted 3-line initials;
some capitals touched in vertical pen strokes; some rubricated
headings.

Hayes 12: Virgil, *Aeneid*, VII, 139–98. Italy (?), c. 1350 (?). 280 x 215
mm. Parchment. Single leaf.

Single column; 200 x 155 mm.; 30 lines; ruled and bounded.

Hayes 13: Cicero, *Paradoxica Stoicorum* (V, 34–41, VI, 46). Italy, late
s. xiv. 275 x 203 mm. Parchment. Bifolium.

Single column; 135 x 90 mm.; 29 lines; ruled and bounded.

Hayes 14: Two leaves from different MSS.
(i) Office of the Dead. s. xiii. 128 x 90 mm. Parchment.

Single column; 80 x 46 mm.; ruled and bounded. Demi-vinet
border on recto, in gilt, blue, and purple, incorporating 3-line
initial *L*; gilt line fillers with designs in blue and red.

(ii) Psalter (?) (Psalms 10: 7–8, 11: 2–9, 12: 1–2). s. xiv (?). 113 x 72 mm. Parchment.

Single column; 56 x 32 mm.; ruled and bounded. 3-line gilt initial *S* on blue and purple, within gilt frame.

Hayes 15: Book of Hours (?). Italy, s. xv. 145 x 68 mm. (all cropped and now mounted). Parchment. Three leaves (the first two paginated '1–4', the third unnumbered).

Single column; 118 x 55 mm. (within gilt frame); 33 lines.

Hayes 16: Two unidentified leaves, each by a different scribe. Italy (?), c. 1300 (?). 115 x 80 mm. Ruled and bounded in ink; numbered '334' and '404' respectively in red, in a contemporary hand. Parchment.

('334'): Double column; each column 90 x 33 mm.; 50 lines to a column; one simple blue painted 2-line initial *S*.

('404'): Double column; each column 90 x 21 mm.; 40 lines to a column; one simple red painted 3-line initial *P* and one 2-line red painted initial *O*; some rubricated headings.

Hayes 17: Breviary. Italy, 1400–50. 118 x 82 mm. Parchment. Single leaf.

Double column; each column 70 x 27 mm.; 23 lines to a column; ruled and bounded. (**BGH**)

Hayes 18: Psalter (?). France (?), s. xv. 172 x 118 mm. Parchment. Two bifolia.

Single column; 80 x 65 mm.; 12 lines.
(i) Psalm 101: 15–25;
(ii) Psalms 101: 25–29, 129: 1–3.

Hayes 19: Unidentified service book. Italy, s. xv (?). 190 x 135 mm. Parchment. Bifolium.

Double column; each column 120 x 38 mm.; 22 lines to a column. Text frequently written in red.

Hayes 20: Psalter (?) / Hours (?). France, s. xv. 120 x 87 mm. Parchment. Single leaf.

Single column; 63 x 48 mm.; ruled in red; 13 lines. Frequent 1- or 2-line gray painted initials on red or gilt ground.

Hayes 21: Book of Hours. France (?), s. xv. 95 x 73 mm. Parchment. Single leaf.

Single column; 53 x 38 mm.; 12 lines. 1-line illuminated initials with green penwork or blue painted initials with red penwork; line fillers of various kinds.

Provenance: Numbered '331' in pencil on lower recto outer margin; numbered '390' in pencil on lower verso outer margin.

Hayes 22: Unidentified service book. France, s. xv. 141 x 111 mm. Parchment. Single leaf.

Single column; 90 x 60 mm.; 14 lines. 1- or 2-line illuminated initials on blue and/or purple ground; line fillers in blue, purple, and gilt with white tracery.

Hayes 23: Book of Hours. France (?), s. xv. 192 x 137 mm. Parchment. Single leaf.

Single column; 101 x 65 mm.; 15 lines; ruled and bounded in red ink.

Hayes 24: Cutting from Antiphonal. Spain (?), s. xvi (?). Parchment.

Initial *H* in blue and white with red and yellow foliate tracery, on a black and silver filigree ground. On verso is noted music in a red stave.

Provenance: A gift to Hayes in 1982 from Mark van Stone.

Hayes 25: Book of Hours. France, late s. xv. 150 x 102 mm. Parchment. Single leaf.

Single column; 150 x 102 mm.; 21 lines; ruled and bounded in red ink.

Hayes 26: Unidentified Latin work. Italy, c. 1450. 172 x 127 mm. Parchment. Bifolium.

Single column; 125 x 80 mm.; 32 lines; ruled and bounded (seemingly originally ruled for double column).

Provenance: Numbered in contemporary hand '212', '213'.

Some annotations on fol. 213v in outer and upper margins in humanistic hand. Presented to Hayes by Jan Tschichold, Berne, Switzerland.

Hayes 27: Breviary (?). Italy, s. xv. 220 x 150 mm. Parchment. Single leaf.

Double column; 150 x 102 mm.; 33 lines to a column. 2-line red painted initials with red penwork or blue with red penwork.

Hayes 28: Book of Hours. Italy, s. xv. 219 x 148 mm. Parchment. Cut into two pieces of irregular size.

Double column; each 160 x 45 mm.; 24 lines to a column; ruled and bounded. Excised miniatures in both columns (approximately 50 x 45 mm. in first; 63 x 45 in second); demi-vinet border in blue, red, green, and gray with some white tracery and gold studding (partly excised); 2/3-line blue painted initials with red penwork.

Hayes 29: Book of Hours. Flanders (?), c. 1440. 190 x 128 mm. Parchment. Single leaf.

Single column; 100 x 60 mm.; 13 lines; ruled and bounded in red. Frequent 1-line illuminated initials infilled in blue on a purple ground, some with tracery.

Provenance: Leaf paginated '281', '282'.

Hayes 30: Breviary. Italy, s. xv. 161 x 116 mm. Parchment. Bifolium.

Double column; each column 88 x 30 mm.; 28 lines to a column.

Hayes 31: Unidentified religious work. France (?), Low Countries (?), s. xv. Fragment of a leaf (now 193 x 100 mm.). Parchment.

Possibly in double column; 31 lines survive; ruled and bounded in plummet.

Hayes 32: Book of Hours. France (?), Belgium (?), 1400. 163 x 85 mm. (severely cropped laterally). Parchment. Single leaf.

Single column; 90 x 65 mm.; ruled for 16 lines (only 12 written); one side of leaf ruled but blank.

Hayes 33: Illuminated initial *L*, perhaps cut from a gradual. Venice (?), Padua (?), c. 1440. 66 x 65 mm. Parchment.

Ruled in red on verso. Gilded and painted in blue with white foliate decoration and green and yellow foliate decoration at all extremities and pink tendrils and blue/white, red/white, and gray/white leaves all extending into the infilling.

Hayes 34: Latin Bible (Josuah 10: 25 – 14: 11). France, s. xiii. 303 x 231 mm. Parchment. Single leaf.

Double column; each column 303 x 231 mm.; 60 lines to a column; ruled and bounded.

Hayes 35: Antiphonal. Spain (?), Italy (?), s. xiv. 226/71 x 258/59 mm. (irregular fragment). Parchment. Single leaf.

Three 4-line staves with square music notation. (**BGH**)

Hayes 37: Antiphonal (?) or gradual (?). Netherlands (?), France (?), s. xv (?). 42 x 42 mm. Parchment. Single leaf.

Painted initial *Q*, infilled in yellow, cut from manuscript with musical notation; 4-line stave ruled in red ink. (**DS**)

Hayes 38: Cutting from antiphonal (?) or gradual (?). Italy, s. xv. 140 x 120 mm. Parchment.

Painted initial *A*, in red, infilled and flourished with blue penwork; horizontal rules in red with musical notation.

Hayes 40: Unidentified document in Italian. Italy, s. xv. 440 x 240 mm. Parchment. Single leaf cropped and folded to form a book wrapper.

Single column; 70 lines; ruled in ink.

Provenance: On otherwise blank side 'Histor. Di Brescia del Lauriolo'.

Hayes 41: Fragment of Latin document. Italy, s. xv. Approximately 205 x 105 mm. Parchment.

Hayes 62: Theological treatise. Italy, s. xv. 223 x 152 mm. Parchment. Single leaf.

Single column; 175 x 100 mm.; 33 lines; ruled and bounded.

Provenance: Leaf folded for use as a binding wrapper (stitching marks visible in spine); '20' on spine.

Hayes 63: Lectionary (?). Italy, s. xiv (?). 158 x 95 mm. Parchment. Single leaf.

Single column; 158 x 95 mm.; 30 lines; ruled and bounded.

Hayes 68 Oversize 1: Prosper, *De activa vita ac contemplativa*. Italy, s. xv. 340 x 235 mm. Parchment. Bifolium + single leaf.

Single column; 205 x 138 mm.; 34 lines; ruled and bounded.

Hayes 72 Oversize 1: Gradual (?). Forty leaves or fragments (mainly fragments), from same MS. Netherlands, s. xv. 375 x 243 mm. Parchment. **(DS)**

Hayes 100: Unidentified Latin work. Italy (?), s. xv (?). Parchment. Binding fragment.

Hayes 101: Eight binding fragments, seemingly from different MSS, all in s. xv hands. Parchment.

Provenance: Given by Elizabeth Kner to Hayes, 26 July 1960.

Hayes 102: Canon law text (?). Northern France (?), s. xiv (?). 151 x 42 mm. Parchment. Binding fragment.

Double column; ruled and bounded in plummet. 3-line historiated initial *S* containing a penwork dragon, infilled with rose, blue, and gilt paint. Traces of illuminated border in gold, purple, and blue. (**DS**)

Hayes 118 Oversize 1: Canon law text (?). Italy, s. xiv. 392 x 280/ 85 mm. Parchment. Two leaves from same MS used as binding fragments.

Double column; each column 237 x 63 mm.; 47 lines to a column. (**DS**)

Hayes 119 Oversize 2: Legal document. France, 1459–61. 410 x 302 mm. Paper. Bifolium (leaves numbered 'xxiii', 'xxx').

Hayes 133 Oversize 1: Mass of the Dead. Germany, 1481. 378 x 276 mm. Parchment. Single leaf.

Double column; each column 265 x 78 mm.; 27 lines to a column.

Provenance: '121' in lower recto margin. (**DS**)

Pl. 4 **Hayes 134**: Glossed Psalter. Northern France, c. 1175. 302 x 198 mm. Parchment. Single leaf.

Triple column; text in center column; glosses in outer ones; 52/53 lines; center column 205 x 75 mm.; outer column (on recto), 210 x 52 mm.; inner column (on recto), 210 x 30 mm.

Provenance: from University of California at Berkeley, Bancroft Library 147; other leaves:

    (i)   one leaf (fol. 53), University of North Carolina, Chapel Hill 100;

    (ii)   eight leaves, Sotheby's, 25 April 1983, lot 13 (to Maggs), presumably the source for (iii)–(iv);

    (iii)   four leaves, Maggs, Bulletin 12 (June 1984), nos. 15–17;

    (iv)   two leaves, Maggs, Bulletin 13 (July 1986), nos. 15–16. (**DS**)

Hayes 135 Oversize 1: Augustine, *Commentary on the Psalms* (*PL* 36, col. 83). England, s. xiii / early s. xiii. 304 x 234 mm. Parchment. Binding fragment.

Double column; each column 266 x 90 mm.; 42 lines to a column; ruled and bounded in plummet. (**DS**)

Hayes 136 Oversize 1: Latin Bible (Amos 5: 15–27). France, early s. xiii. 348 x 245 mm. Parchment. Single leaf.

Triple column; text in center column; glosses in outer ones; 52/53 lines; main column 200 x 50 mm.; outer columns 27 x 200 mm. and 40 x 200 mm. Blue or red painted 2-line initials. Paraffs in blue or red.

Provenance:
- (i)   one leaf, Sotheby's, 25 April 1983, lot 19 (now in a private collection in California);
- (ii)   one leaf, Sotheby's, 26 November 1985, lot 50 (to Quaritch). (**DS**)

S. Harrison Thomson Manuscripts

S. Harrison Thomson (1895–1975) taught at the University of Colorado from 1936 until his retirement. He wrote extensively about medieval manuscripts and palaeography, most notably in his *Latin Bookhands of the Later Middle Ages* (Cambridge, 1969). Thomson developed a substantial collection of medieval manuscripts many of which were subsequently acquired by the Beinecke Library, New Haven, between 1967 and 1970: their MSS 311, 322, 352, 368, 371, 373, 378, 379, 383, 385, 392, 432, 453, 470, 471, 472, 473, 474, all come from his collection. UCB possesses a collection he assembled of 46 fragments, of which two, 27, 29, are printed leaves from incunables. It was purchased from Bernard Rosenthal of San Francisco between 1973 and 1982.

For some account of Thomson's career see Lubomyr R. Wynar, *S. Harrison Thomson Bio-Bibliography*. University of Colorado Libraries. Bio-Bibliographical Series: No. 1 (Boulder, 1963), and the obituary in *Speculum* 51 (1976): 578–80.

Thomson 1: Latin Bible (table of contents from Genesis to Epistle to Titus). s. xiii / s. xvi. 193 x 167 mm. Parchment. Single leaf. Binding fragment.

Double column; each column 170 x 65 mm.; c. 33 lines to each column; bounded. Offset on verso from unidentified text in s. xi script to which this fragment was once affixed as part of the binding.

Provenance: Pencilled '3' on bottom left hand corner of recto. (**MF**)

Thomson 2: Joannes Scotus Erigena, *Homilia in prologum Euangelii secundum Ioannem* (*PL* 122, col. 287). s. xi. 282 x 185/212 mm. Parchment. Single leaf (torn).

Single column; 142 x 102 mm.; 15 lines.

Provenance: Several stitching holes suggest that the leaf was used as a binding wrapper at some point. (**MF**)

Thomson 3: Lectionary (?). Italy, s. xi/xii (?). 210 x 305 mm. Parchment. Binding fragment.

Double column; each column 100 mm. wide; 22 lines to a column. Verso blank. (**MF**)

Thomson 4: Lectionary. Germany, s. xi/xii. 240 x 235 mm. Parchment. Bifolium, cropped and shaped as if to form a wrapper binding.

Single column; 223 x 150 mm.; 28 lines. Occasional 5–6 line painted initials.

Provenance: Note in gutter in pencil 'Ansagr 11412 | M N7.—' and (in a different hand) 'Lectionarium 506 357'. (**MF**)

Thomson 5: Missal (?). Germany, s. xi/xii (overwritten in s. xiv cursive script). 282 x 229 mm. Parchment. Bifolium (cropped).

Single column; 187 x 116 mm.; 23 lines.

Provenance: Formerly in the collection of E. A. Lowe. Notes on fol. 1r in pencil 'I/223' and '77.H'. (**MF**)

Thomson 6: Prayers (?). France, s. xii. c. 155 x 70 mm. Parchment. Fragment; parts of 19 lines. (**MF**)

Thomson 7: Religious text (?). Germany, s. xii. 145 x 71 mm. Parchment. Fragment; parts of 17 lines. (**MF**)

Thomson 8: Unidentified Latin text. France (?), Germany (?), s. xii. 222 x 152 mm. Parchment. Fragment of single leaf used as binder's waste.

Double column; each column 80 mm. wide; 27 lines surviving in each column. (**MF**)

Thomson 9: Breviary. Germany, s. xii. 315 x 230 mm. Parchment. Bifolium.

Single column; 180 x 115 mm.; 34 lines to a column. (**MF**)

Thomson 10: Latin Bible (4 Kings 6: 33 – 10: 5). France, s. xiii. 205 x 140 mm. Parchment. Single leaf.

Double column; each column 170 x 52 mm.; 65 lines to a column; ruled and bounded in plummet. Running title and chapter numbers alternately blue and red.

Provenance: '99' in modern pencil on top right hand corner recto; 'xcix' in ink in medieval hand. (**JM**)

Thomson 11: St. Jerome, *De essencia divinitatis Domini et de invisibilitate et immensitate eius* (*PL* 30, col. 175). Germany, mid s. xiii. 247 x 178 mm. Parchment. Bifolium (cropped at top).

Double column; each column 90 x 71 mm.; 32/33 lines to each column; ruled and bounded in plummet. Prick marks visible. Some simple red painted initials; some rubrication. (**MF**)

Thomson 12: Latin Bible (Wisdom 13: 3 – 17: 9). France, s. xiii. 295 x 195 mm. Parchment. Single leaf.

Double column; each column 190 x 50 mm.; 63 lines to a column; ruled and bounded in drypoint. (**MF**)

Thomson 13: Unidentified devotional text. France, s. xiii. 188 x 150 mm. Parchment. Bifolium (second leaf cropped in bottom right hand corner).

Double column; each column 160 x 50 mm.; 41 lines to a column; ruled and bounded in black ink. (**MF**)

Thomson 14: Peter Damian, Commentary (?) on Genesis (*PL* 198, col. 1109). s. xiii. 290 x 199 mm. Parchment. Single leaf.

Double column; each column 210 x 50 mm.; 53 lines to a column. Blue or red painted initials of varying size. (**MF**)

Thomson 15: Canon law text (?); Gratian (?), Decretum (?). France, s. xiii. 230 x 167/85 mm. Parchment. Bifolium used as a pastedown.

Double column; each column 210 x 65 mm.; 49 lines to a column.

Provenance: 'R7' pencilled on bottom lower left hand corner of fol. 2r.

Thomson 16: Bible commentary (?). Germany (?), late s. xiii. 150 x 116 mm. Parchment. Single leaf.

Single column; 120 x 95 mm.; 26 lines.

Provenance: Seemingly used as binder's waste. (**MF**)

Thomson 17: Scholastic text (?) citing Plato and Aristotle. France, second half of s. xiii. 245 x 185 mm. Parchment. Single leaf.

Double column; each column 225 x 72 mm.; 39 lines to a column. 4-line blue and red painted initial *Q*, infilled with red penwork, with elaborate descender. (**MF**)

Thomson 18: Legal text (?). Italy, s. xiii/xiv. 282 x 187 mm. Parchment. Single leaf.

Double column; each column 255 x 81 mm.; 57 lines to a column; ruled in plummet. (**JM**)

Thomson 19: Missal. Germany, s. xiv. 210 x 153 mm. Parchment. Fragment of much larger leaf.

Double column; one of which is only fragmentary; the other is 100 mm. wide; 15 lines survive; ruled and bounded in drypoint. (**MF**)

Thomson 20: Missal. Germany, s. xiv. 308 x 93 mm. Parchment (one column cut from a much larger leaf).

Single column; 21 lines; bounded.

Thomson 21: Glossed civil law text. Italy, s. xiv. 281 x 188 mm. Parchment. Single leaf.

Three columns: single central column of primary text (162 x 101 mm.), ruled and bounded; 28 lines to a column. The inner and outer columns are of commentary, extending above and below the text in a smaller cursive hand. 3-line red painted *P*; occasional rubrication. (**MF**)

Thomson 22: Benedictional. Germany, s. xiv. 288 x 194 mm. Parchment. Single leaf (cropped).

Single column; 214 x 142 mm.; 25 lines; ruled and bounded in plummet. (**MF**)

Thomson 23: Possibly from Bede, *Homiliae subditae* (*PL* 94, col. 324) or *In Euangelium Lucae* (*PL* 92, col. 315). Germany, s. xiv. 235 x 180 mm. Parchment. Single leaf.

Single column; 180 x 127 mm.; 33 lines. (**MF**)

Thomson 24: Canon Law text (?). Northern France (?), Italy (?), early s. xiv. 204 x 153 mm. Parchment. Fragment of single leaf (cropped at bottom).

Single column; 193 x 93 mm.; 41 lines; ruled and bounded in plummet. (**JM**)

Thomson 25: Unidentified text, possibly scholastic. France (?), Italy (?), s. xiv. 321 x 234 mm. Parchment. Single leaf.

Double column; each column 212 x 67 mm.; 46 lines to a column; ruled and bounded in plummet. 2-line painted initials in blue with red penwork, red with green penwork; some rubrication. (**JM**)

Thomson 26: Sermon text (?). Germany, s. xiv. 318 x 231 mm. Parchment. Single leaf (probably binding fragment).

Double column; each column 246 x 80 mm.; 40 lines to a column; ruled and bounded in ink. (**MF**)

Thomson 28: Breviary. Flanders, s. xiv. 224 x 148 mm. Parchment. Bifolium (one leaf ruled but blank).

Single column; 152 x 82 mm.; 31 lines; ruled and bounded in plummet. (**JM**)

Thomson 30: Calendar page from Book of Hours (headed 'September' on recto, 'October' on verso). England, s. xv. 125 x 85 mm. Parchment. Single leaf.

Single column; 87 x 54 mm.; ruled and bounded in black/brown. 2-line gilt initials at beginning of each month infilled in blue or purple with white tracery; some saints' names rubricated. (**BP**)

Thomson 31: Cicero, *De amicitia* (26. 100–27. 104). Italy, s. xv. 205 x 129 mm. Parchment. Single leaf.

Single column; 135 x 92 mm.; 27 lines; ruled and bounded in drypoint. Occasional 1- or 2-line blue or red painted initials. (**BGH**)

Thomson 32: Book of Hours (?). Netherlands, s. xv. 130 x 93 mm. Parchment. Bifolium.

Single column; 90 x 63 mm.; 22 lines; ruled in ink. Frequent 1- or 2-line blue or red painted initials.

Provenance: 'R' at bottom right hand corner of first leaf; '74' in modern pencil on recto of second leaf. (**BGH**)

Thomson 33: Missal. Germany, s. xv. 325 x 240 mm. Parchment. Bifolium.

Double column; each column 265 x 83 mm.; 36 lines to a column; ruled and bounded in ink. Some green and red painted initials (2–4 lines); frequent border flourishes in green and red. (**BGH**)

Thomson 34: Notarial letter. Italy (Perugia), s. xv. 339 x 215 mm. Parchment. Single leaf (very damaged). **(BGH)**

Thomson 35: Missal (from Requiem Mass). England, s. xv. 293 x 195/200 mm. Parchment. Single leaf.

Double column; each column 200 x 60 mm.; 36 lines to a column; ruled and bounded in ink. 2-line gilt initials on blue or purple ground, infilled in contrasting color, with white tracery; frequent rubrication. **(JM)**

Thomson 36: Notarial letter (for Charles, Duke of Savoy). Italy, s. xv. 301 x 215 mm. Paper. **(BGH)**

Thomson 37: Breviary. England, s. xv. 140 x 100 mm. Parchment. Bifolium.

Single column; 97 x 72 mm.; 18 lines; ruled and bounded in ink.

Provenance: fols. 1v, 2r in lower margins: 'A boke of receipts from my Brother Cole 1626'. **(JM)**

Thomson 38: Unidentified text (with references to Justinus, Bede, Isidore and Hugh of St. Victor). France (?), s. xiii. 315 x 245/50 mm. Parchment. Bifolium.

Double column; each column 235 x 75 mm.; 64 lines to a column; ruled and bounded in ink. 1–2 line blue or red painted initials. **(BGH)**

Thomson 39: Canon Law text (?). France (?), s. xiv. 212 x 166 mm. (cropped at top). Parchment. Single leaf.

Double column; each column 182 x 58 mm.; 48 lines to a column; ruled and bounded in plummet. 2/3-line blue or red painted initials. **(BGH)**

Thomson 40: Unidentified text. Italy (?), late s. xiii. 246 x 180 mm. Parchment. Single leaf (cropped, possibly binding fragment).

Double column of text, surrounded by commentary. 2/3-line blue or red painted initials; some rubrication. (**BGH**)

Thomson 41: Unidentified text (with references to Justinus, Bede, and Isidore). England (?), s. xiv. 260 x 200 mm. Parchment. Single leaf.

Double column; each column 195 x 60 mm.; 34 lines to a column; ruled and bounded in plummet. Prick marks visible. Names of authorities rubricated in outer margin. (**BGH**)

Thomson 42: Philosophical text (?). France (?), s. xiv. Binding fragment of bifolium, 169 x 88 mm. and 125 x 135 mm. Parchment. (**BGH**)

Thomson 43: Missal (?). French (?), s. xv. 172 x 200 mm. Parchment. Part of single leaf with stub of conjugate leaf.

Double column; each column 142 x 70 mm. (heavily cropped); ruled in ink. (**BGH**)

Thomson 44: Breviary. France (?), s. xv. Leaves have been cut horizontally, overlapped, and glued together again. Approx. 111 x 93 mm. Parchment. Bifolium.

Single column; 81 x 53 mm.; 13 lines; ruled and bounded in ink. (**BGH**)

Thomson 45: Breviary (?). France (?), England (?), s. xiv. 172 x 43 mm. Parchment. Column of single leaf.

Single column; 108 x 30 mm.; 31 lines. 2-line blue or red painted initials; some rubrication. (**BGH**)

Thomson 46 Oversize: Latin Bible (Interpretation of Hebrew Names). Italy, s. xiii. 303 x 223 mm. Parchment. Bifolium.

Triple column; each column 212 x 53 mm.; 56 lines to a column; ruled and bounded in plummet. 1-line painted initials, alternately blue or red. (**BGH**)

Department of Fine Arts
Colorado Collection

The Colorado Collection of the Department of Fine Arts at UCB contains a small number of leaves that have been included here.

MS 57.218: Book of Hours. Normandy, c. 1430. 138 x 104 mm. (cropped). Parchment. Single leaf. Framed under glass.

Single column; 108 x 68 mm.; recto ruled and bounded in brown ink for 21 lines. Miniature of St. James and St. Philip facing each other on verso.

Provenance: From the Tarleton Hours executed by a follower of the Rohan Master; complete MS sold Christie's, 3 July 1951, lot 50 (to Maggs) and thirty-five leaves with miniatures subsequently removed and sold separately, including **MS 57.218** and **MS 57.219**, both purchased by UCB in 1957; this leaf was sold Sotheby's, 4 May 1953, lot 42, and formed fol. 48 of the original manuscript. The bulk of the rest of the manuscript (ff. 125) was sold again Sotheby's, 20 June 1989, lot 58, with a full analysis of the original complete manuscript, to which we are greatly indebted; we note the sale of the following leaves since then:

(i)   four leaves, Sotheby's, 19 June 1990 (Collection of the late Eric Korner), lots 28–31 (hymn to the Holy Cross: fol. 42; St. James the Greater: fol. 47; St. Martin: fol. 56; St. Christopher: fol. 52);

(ii)   one leaf, Sotheby's, 21 June 1993 (Alan Thomas sale), lot 25 (St. Nicholas: fol. 55);

(iii)   one leaf, Sotheby's, 23 June 1998, lot 26 (previously
       Maggs, Bulletin 3, 1965, no. 27) (St. Julian: fol. 55);
(iv)   one leaf, Maggs, Catalogue 1283 (1999), no. 9 (Thomas
       à Becket: fol. 53). (**MF**)

MS 57.219: Book of Hours. Normandy, c. 1430. 140 x 99 mm.
(cropped). Parchment. Single leaf. Framed under glass.

Single column; 100 x 67 mm.; recto ruled and bounded in
brown ink for 20 lines. Miniature of St. Ursinus on verso.

Provenance: Originally fol. 58 in the complete manuscript; see
further **MS 57.218**. (**MF**)

MS 67.332: Antiphonal. Italy (?), s. xv. 352 x 231 mm. Parchment.
Single leaf.

4-line staves with square notation. 161 x 155 mm. Ruled in red
ink. Historiated initial on recto, depicting a nimbed and bearded
Christ on a bright orange ground.

Provenance: Rubricated quire signature 'hiii' on recto. Gift of
Mrs. Alfred Kressler. (**BGH**)

MS 68.352: Latin Bible (1 Corinthians 10: 3 – 10: 10). France, s. xiii.
375 x 268 mm. Parchment. Single leaf.

Double columns; each column 214 x 64 mm.; 34 lines to a
column; ruled and bounded in plummet. 2-line blue or red painted initials with penwork in alternating color; 1-line blue or red
painted initials; some underlining in red.

Provenance: Gift of Mrs. Alfred Kressler. (**BGH**)

MS 86.1911P: Latin Bible (end of Jerome's Preface to Matthew,
Matthew 1: 1–24). France, s. xiii^2. 145 x 104 mm. (approximately:
it was only possible to examine leaf under glass). Parchment.
Single leaf. Framed under glass.

Double column; each column 100 x 35 mm.; 51 lines to a column; ruled and bounded in plummet. 22-line historiated initial *L*
depicting Jesse in a red robe over a white gown reclining on a

white couch. Branches of Tree of Jesse depicting Solomon, David, and Jesus.

Provenance: see further UCB **MS 284**. (**MF**)

MS 91.1: Latin Bible (Judges 20: 31 – Ruth 1: 15). France, s. xiii. 289 x 86 mm. Parchment. Single leaf (cut in half lengthwise).

Single column; 192 x 57 mm.; 50 lines; ruled and bounded in plummet. 16-line historiated initial *I* at beginning of Book of Ruth; upper compartment contains a male figure carrying a staff, wearing an orange pointed cap and rose-brown garments on a gold rectilinear ground; the lower compartment contains a woman in blue garments wearing a white headdress with her hand on a child's head, on a gold rectilinear ground.

Provenance: *Olim* Feldman 18; sold by him to UCB, 17 May 1991 for $3,500. (**BGH**)

MS 91.2.1: Latin Bible (Jerome Prologue to Bible). France, s. xiii. 145 x 210 mm. Parchment. Single leaf.

Double column; each column 141 x 43 mm.; 49 lines to a column. Demi-vinet border incorporating historiated initial *F* (6-line) of figure standing at lectern.

Provenance: Donated by John Feldman in May 1991. (**BGH**)

Indices

GENERAL INDEX
(Throughout, the Department of Fine Arts
is cited as 'Fine Arts'.)

Anonymi sermones de tempore, MS 80

Antiphonal, MS 334 OS, Ege 27, Hayes 24, Hayes 35, Hayes 37, Hayes 38 (?), Fine Arts MS 67.332

Aquinas, Thomas, *Commentary on the Sentences*, Ege 40

Augustine, *In Iohannis Evangelium tractatus*, MS 333 OS, *Commentary on the Psalms*, Hayes 135 Oversize 1

(Pseudo) Augustine, MS 1

Aurora, Ege 7

Bede, Thomson 23

Benedictional, Thomson 22

Bible, MS 284, MS 285, MS 287, MS 291, MS 299, MS 300, MS 309, MS 314, MS 317, MS 318, MS 319, MS 320, MS 323, MS 324, MS 325, MS 326, MS 328, MS 345, MS 356, Ege 1, Ege 5, Ege 6, Ege 9, Ege 11, Ege 13, Ege 14, Ege 19, Ege 44, Hayes 4, Hayes 34, Hayes 136 Oversize 1, Thomson 1, Thomson 10, Thomson 12, Thomson 46, Fine Arts MS 68.352, Fine Arts MS 86.1911P, Fine Arts MS 91.1, Fine Arts MS 91.2.1

Bible commentary (?), Thomson 16

Breviary, Ege 16, Ege 18, Ege 23, Ege 32, Hayes 17, Hayes 27 (?), Hayes 30, Thomson 9, Thomson 28, Thomson 37, Thomson 44, Thomson 45 (?)

Lebaude, Gautier, MS 321
Lectionary, Ege 3, Hayes 63, Thomson 3 (?), Thomson 4
Legal document, Hayes 119 Oversize 2
Legal text (?), Thomson 18, Thomson 21
Letter, MS 348
Livy, *History of Rome*, Ege 39
Lombard, Peter, MS 321

Martyrum (?), Hayes 11
Mass of the Dead, Hayes 133 Oversize 1
Memorandum of payments, MS 339
Missal, Ege 2, Ege 15, Ege 22, Ege 26, Ege 33, Ege 38, Ege 49,
     Thomson 5 (?), Thomson 19, Thomson 20, Thomson 33,
     Thomson 35
Music, Hayes 2

Notarial documents, MS 352
Notarial letter, Thomson 34, Thomson 36

Office of the Dead, Hayes 14

Philosophical text (?), Thomson 42
Prayers (?), Thomson 6
Prosper, *De activa vita ac contemplativa*, Hayes 68 Oversize 1
Psalter (?), MS 327, Ege 4, Ege 10, Ege 12, Ege 17, Ege 20, Ege 32,
     Ege 34, Ege 42, Hayes 1, Hayes 14, Hayes 18 (?), Hayes 20 (?),
     Hayes 134

Quaestiones, MS 332

Religious text (?), Thomson 7
Riga, Petrus, *Aurora*, Ege 7

Scholastic text (?), Thomson 17
Sermon (?), Thomson 26

Service book, Hayes 19, Hayes 22

Tarleton Hours, Fine Arts MS 57.218, Fine Arts MS 57.219
Terence, Hayes 9
Theological treatise, Hayes 62

Virgil, *Aeneid*, Hayes 12

INDEX OF MANUSCRIPTS BY DATE
(Manuscripts not securely dated to a single century
are given more than one entry.)

s. ix: MS 355

s. xi: Hayes 10, Thomson 2, Thomson 3, Thomson 4, Thomson 5

s. xii: MS 314, Ege 1, Ege 2, Ege 3, Ege 4, Hayes 2, Hayes 11, Hayes 134, Thomson 3, Thomson 4, Thomson 5, Thomson 6, Thomson 7, Thomson 8, Thomson 9

s. xiii: MS 80, MS 284, MS 285, MS 287, MS 291, MS 299, MS 300, MS 309, MS 316, MS 317, MS 318, MS 319, MS 320, MS 321, MS 323, MS 324, MS 325, MS 326, MS 327, MS 328, MS 332, MS 333 OS, MS 341, Ege 5, Ege 6, Ege 7, Ege 8, Ege 9, Ege 10, Ege 11, Ege 12, Ege 13, Ege 14, Ege 15, Ege 16, Ege 17, Ege 18, Hayes 14(i), Hayes 34, Hayes 135 Oversize 1, Hayes 136, Thomson 1, Thomson 10, Thomson 11, Thomson 12, Thomson 13, Thomson 14, Thomson 15, Thomson 16, Thomson 17, Thomson 18, Thomson 38, Thomson 40, Thomson 46, Fine Arts MS 68.352, Fine Arts MS 86.1911P, Fine Arts MS 91.1, Fine Arts MS 91.2.1

s. xiv: MS 102, MS 308, MS 332, MS 345, MS 348, MS 356, Ege 19, Ege 20, Ege 21, Ege 22, Ege 23, Ege 24, Ege 26, Hayes 4, Hayes 13, Hayes 14(ii), Hayes 16, Hayes 35, Hayes 102,

Hayes 118 Oversize 1, Thomson 1, Thomson 18, Thomson 19, Thomson 20, Thomson 21, Thomson 22, Thomson 23, Thomson 24, Thomson 25, Thomson 26, Thomson 28, Thomson 39, Thomson 41, Thomson 42, Thomson 45

s. xv: MS 1, MS 313, MS 315, MS 322, MS 334 OS, MS 338, MS 340, MS 344, MS 349, MS 350, MS 351, MS 352, Ege 27, Ege 28, Ege 31, Ege 32, Ege 33, Ege 34, Ege 35, Ege 36, Ege 37, Ege 38, Ege 39, Ege 40, Ege 41, Ege 42, Ege 43, Ege 44, Ege 45, Ege 46, Hayes 1, Hayes 3, Hayes 5, Hayes 6, Hayes 7, Hayes 8, Hayes 9, Hayes 12, Hayes 15, Hayes 17, Hayes 18, Hayes 19, Hayes 20, Hayes 21, Hayes 22, Hayes 23, Hayes 25, Hayes 26, Hayes 27, Hayes 28, Hayes 29, Hayes 30, Hayes 31, Hayes 32, Hayes 33, Hayes 37, Hayes 38, Hayes 40, Hayes 41, Hayes 62, Hayes 63, Hayes 68, Hayes 72 Oversize 1, Hayes 101, Hayes 119 Oversize 2, Hayes 133 Oversize 1, Thomson 30, Thomson 31, Thomson 32, Thomson 33, Thomson 34, Thomson 35, Thomson 36, Thomson 37, Thomson 43, Thomson 44, Fine Arts MS 57.218, Fine Arts MS 57.219, Fine Arts MS 67.332

s. xvi: Ege 49, Hayes 24, Hayes 100

INDEX OF MANUSCRIPTS BY COUNTRY

Austria: Hayes 11 (?)

England: MS 324 (?), MS 339, MS 340, MS 348, MS 349, MS 350, Ege 6, Ege 7, Ege 8, Ege 13, Ege 17, Ege 24, Hayes 135 Oversize 1, Thomson 30, Thomson 35 (?), Thomson 41 (?), Thomson 45 (?)

France: MS 284, MS 285, MS 287, MS 291, MS 299, MS 300, MS 308, MS 309, MS 313, MS 314, MS 316, MS 317, MS 318, MS 319, MS 320, MS 322, MS 324 (?), MS 325, MS 326, MS 327, MS 332, MS 345, MS 355 (?), MS 356, Ege 4, Ege 5, Ege 9, Ege 12, Ege 14, Ege 15, Ege 16, Ege 18, Ege 21, Ege 23, Ege 26, Ege 28, Ege 29, Ege 30, Ege 35, Ege 36, Ege 38, Ege 41, Ege 45, Ege 46, Hayes 3, Hayes 4 (?), Hayes 5, Hayes 6, Hayes 7, Hayes 15, Hayes 18, Hayes 20, Hayes 21, Hayes 22, Hayes 23 (?), Hayes 25, Hayes 29, Hayes 31, Hayes 32 (?), Hayes 34, Hayes 102 (?), Hayes 119 Oversize 2, Hayes 134, Hayes 136 Oversize 1, Thomson 6, Thomson 8 (?), Thomson 10, Thomson 12, Thomson 13 (?), Thomson 15, Thomson 17, Thomson 24 (?), Thomson 25 (?), Thomson 39 (?), Thomson 42 (?), Thomson 43 (?), Thomson 44 (?), Thomson 45 (?), Fine Arts 57.218, Fine Arts 57.219, Fine Arts 68.352, Fine Arts 86.1911P, Fine Arts 91.1, Fine Arts 91.2.1

Germany: MS 350, MS 355 (?), Ege 10, Ege 22, Ege 33, Ege 42, Ege

49, Hayes 133 Oversize 1, Thomson 4 (?), Thomson 5, Thomson 7, Thomson 9 (?), Thomson 11, Thomson 16, Thomson 19, Thomson 20, Thomson 22, Thomson 23 (?), Thomson 26, Thomson 33

Italy: MS 1, MS 102, MS 328, MS 333 OS, MS 334, MS 341, MS 344, Ege 3, Ege 11, Ege 19, Ege 27, Ege 32, Ege 34, Ege 37, Ege 39, Ege 40, Hayes 1, Hayes 2, Hayes 8, Hayes 9, Hayes 10, Hayes 12, Hayes 13, Hayes 16, Hayes 17, Hayes 19, Hayes 27, Hayes 28, Hayes 30, Hayes 33, Hayes 35, Hayes 36 (?), Hayes 37, Hayes 38, Hayes 40, Hayes 62, Hayes 63, Hayes 118 Oversize 1, Thomson 3, Thomson 18, Thomson 21, Thomson 24 (?), Thomson 25 (?), Thomson 31, Thomson 34, Thomson 36, Thomson 38 (?), Thomson 40 (?), Thomson 46, Fine Arts 67.332 (?)

Netherlands: MS 315, MS 338, Ege 20, Ege 43, Hayes 4 (?), Hayes 72, Thomson 28, Thomson 32, Thomson 37

Spain: MS 352, Ege 2, Hayes 36 (?)

Switzerland: Ege 1

PROVENANCE

(This does not include named collections, Ege, Hayes, Thomson.)

Almagest Atelier, MS 309, MS 318
Arundel, Stephen, MS 299

Bancroft Library, University of California, Berkeley, MS 147,
     Hayes 134
Beatty, Sir Chester, MS 320
Bergendal Collection, Ege 22
Brandt, Mortimer, MS 316
Brölemann, Henri Auguste, Ege 15

Caxton Club of Chicago, Hayes 10
Christie's, Fine Arts MS 57.218, Fine Arts MS 57.219
Claxton, dame Isabell de, MS 348
Culton, Alan, MS 313

Dawson's (Los Angeles), Hayes 9
Dominican Painter, MS 320
Drouffeld, John, MS 349
Drouffeld, Thomas, MS 349

Ege, Otto F., Hayes 8 (?), Hayes 9

Feldman, John, MS 284, MS 285, MS 287, MS 299, MS 300, MS
     308, MS 309, MS 313, MS 315, MS 316, MS 317, MS 318, MS

Proski, D., MS 309

Quaritch, MS 317, MS 318, MS 344, MS 348, MS 349, MS 350, MS
    351

Sanvito, Bartolomeo, Hayes 1
Schuster Gallery, MS 321
Sotheby's, MS 291, MS 299, MS 320, MS 321, MS 345, MS 355, Ege
    6, Ege 14, Ege 22, Ege 39, Hayes 9, Fine Arts 57.218, Fine Arts
    57.219
St Albans, MS 345
Swann Galleries, MS 300, MS 313

Thomas, Alan, MS 102, Fine Arts 57.218
Thorpe, Ege 41
Tschichold, Jan, Hayes 26

Ursuleo, Pietro, Hayes 8

Vandersall, Amy, MS 345

Witten, L., MS 314

Plates

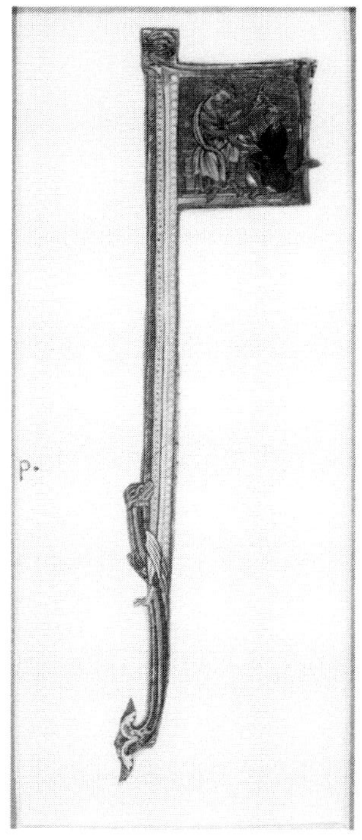

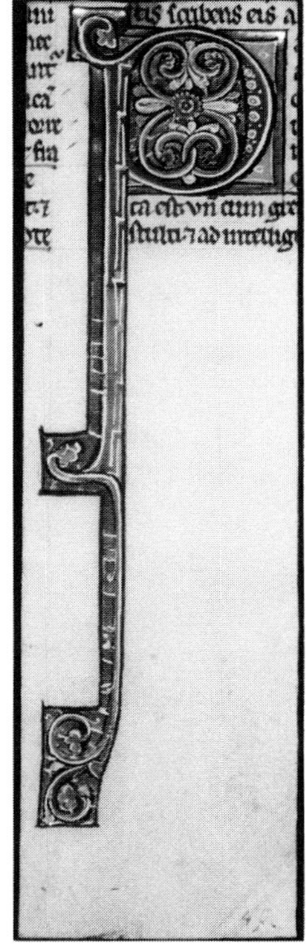

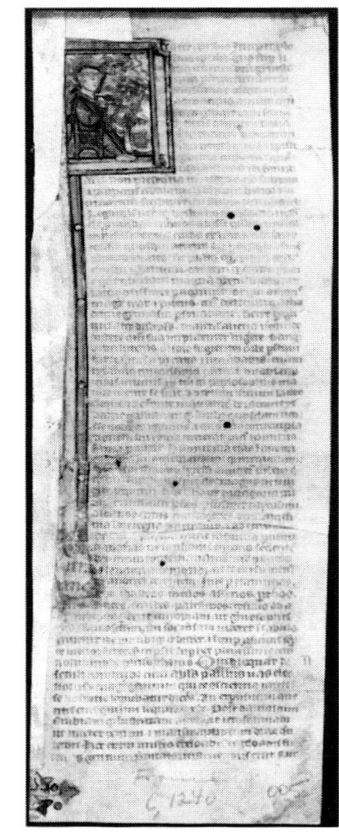

Plate 1: MS 316, Bible Leaf cut F § MS 321, Initial P from Peter Lombard § MS 325, Frater Leaf

Plate 2. MS 309, detail § MS 309, Bible leaf, Psalm 51 § MS 314, Dragon Leaf

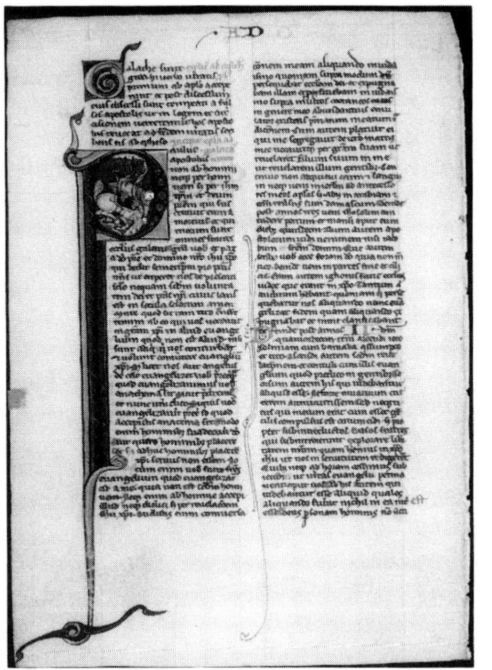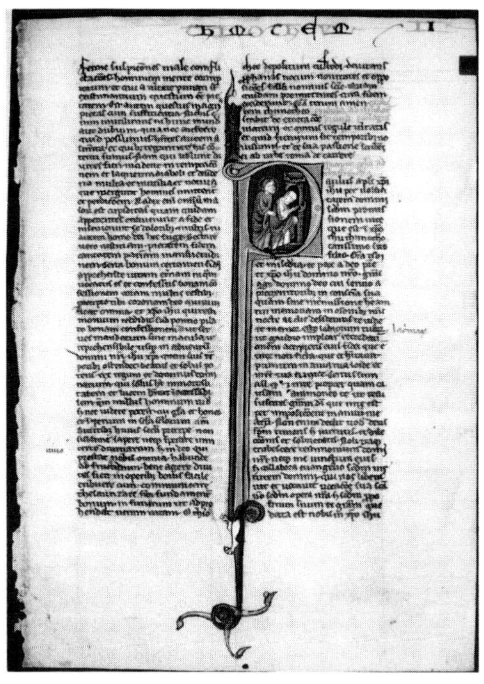

Plate 3. MS 284, Bible Leaf, Paul's conversion § MS 284, detail § MS 285, Blind Paul

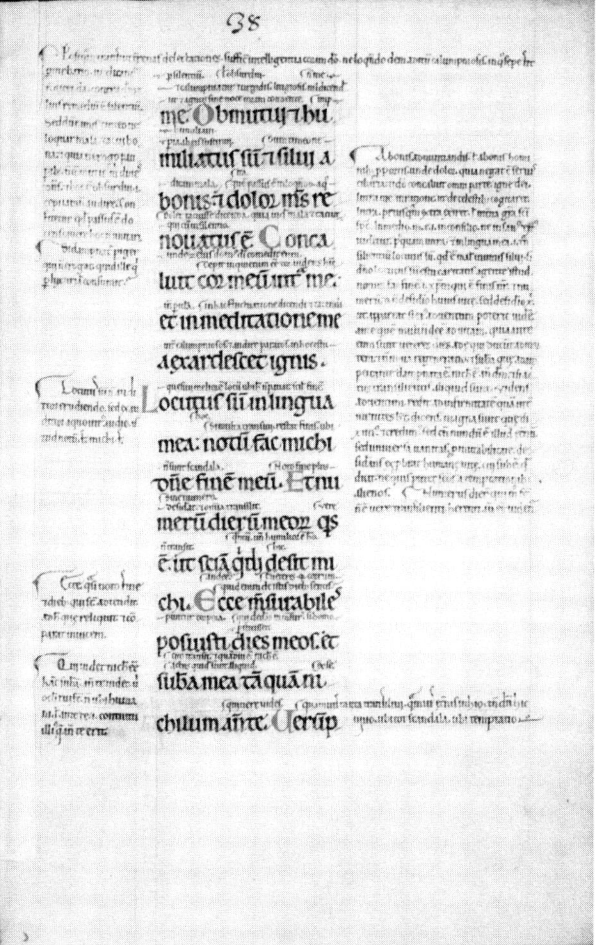

Plate 4. Hayes 134, Psalter, glossed

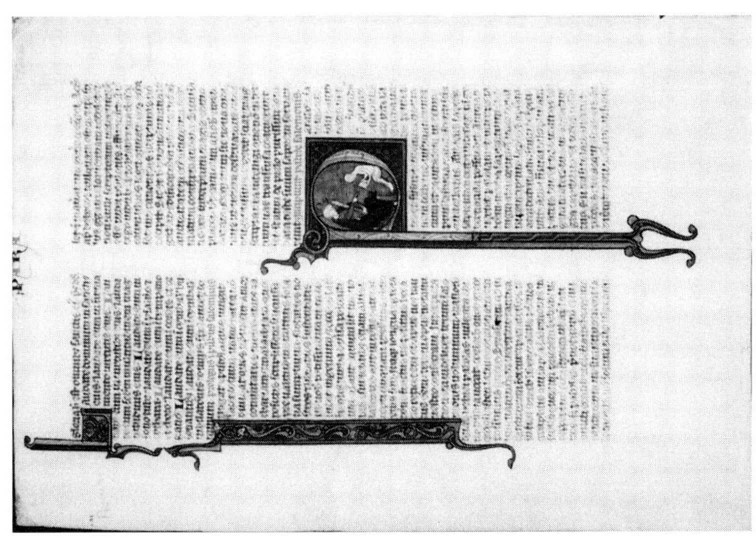

Plate 5: MS 320, Bible Leaf, Solomon & Rehoboam

§   MS 320, Detail

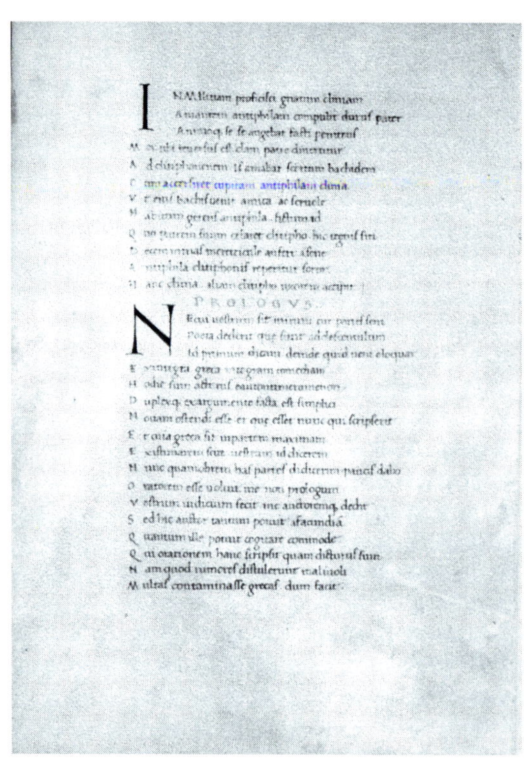

In militiam profectus gnatum Cliniam
Amantem antiphilam compulit durus pater
Animoque se se angebat facti paenitens
Mox ut reversus est clam patre divertitur
Ad clitiphonem is amabat scortum bachidem
Cum accersivit cupitam antiphilam clinia
Ut eius bachis venit amica ac servolae
Habitum gerens antiphila factum id
Quo patrem suum celaret clitipho hic technis
Exercitatus meretricule auferri a sene
Antiphila clitiphonis reperitur soror
Hanc clinia aliam clitipho uxorem accipit

PROLOGVS

Ne cui vestrum sit mirum cur partes seni
Poeta dederit que sunt adulescentium
Id primum dicam deinde quod veni eloquar
Ex integra greca integram comoediam
Hodie sum acturus heautontimorumenon
Duplexque ex argumento facta est simplici
Novam ostendi esse et que esset nunc qui scripserit
Et cuia greca sit ni partem maximam
Existimarem scire vestrum id dicerem
Nunc quamobrem has partes didicerim paucis dabo
Oratorem esse voluit me non prologum
Vestrum iudicium fecit me actoremque dedit
Sed hic actor tantum poterit a facundia
Quantum ille potuit cogitare commode
Qui orationem hanc scripsit quam dicturus sum
Nam quod rumores distulerunt malivoli
Multas contaminasse grecas dum facit

Plate 6. Hayes 9, Terence, Comedy

Plate 7: MS 287, Bible Leaf, Baruch   §   MS 317, Job on dung heap   §   MS 318, Decorated initial D

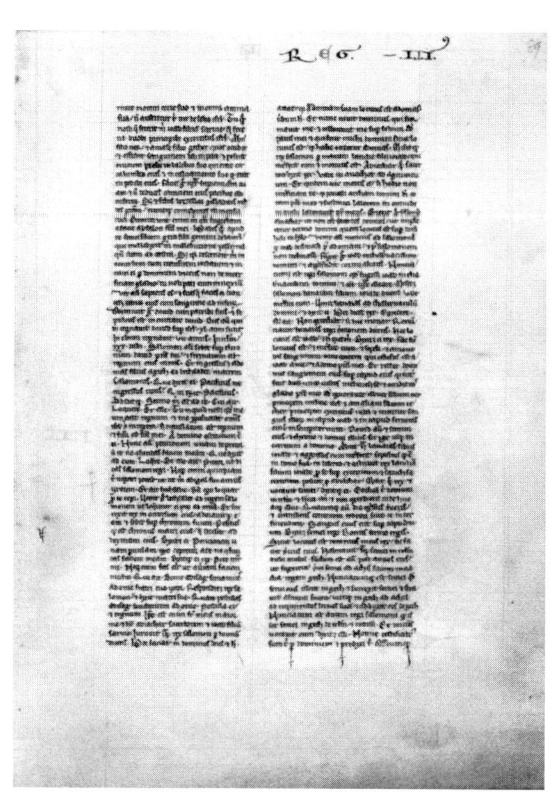

Plate 8. Ege 6, Cambridge Bible

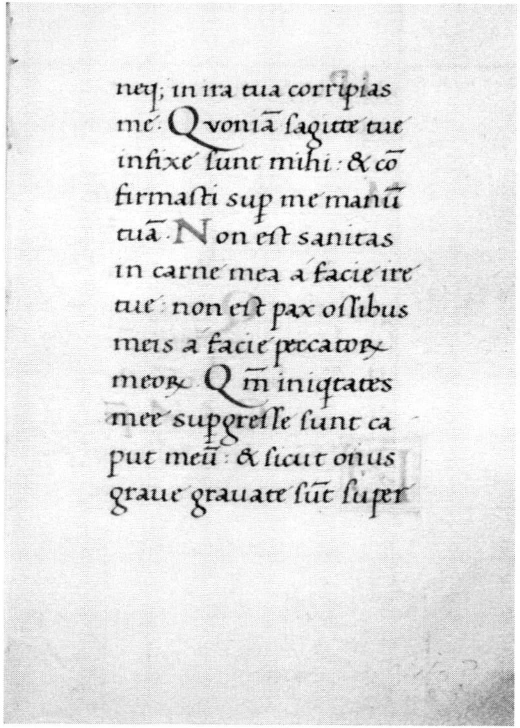

neq; in ira tua corripias
me. Quoniã sagitte tue
infixe sunt mihi: & cõ
firmasti sup me manũ
tuã. Non est sanitas
in carne mea a facie ire
tue: non est pax ossibus
meis a facie peccator*
meor* Qm iniqtates
mee supgresse sunt ca
put meũ: & sicut onus
graue grauate sũt super

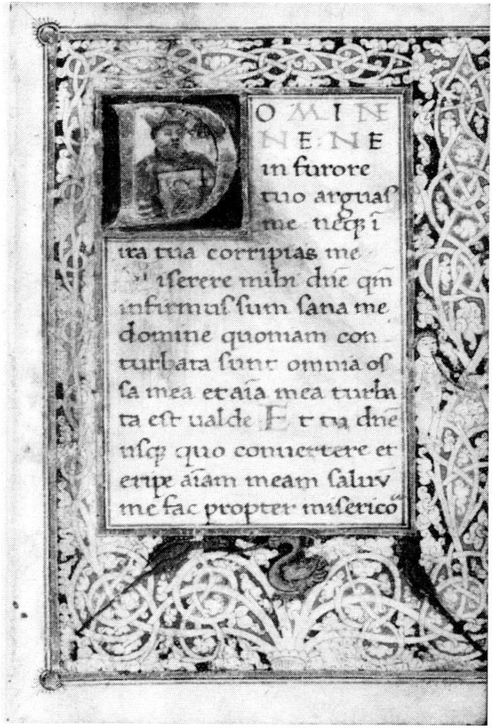

DOMI
NE NE
in furore
tuo arguas
me neq; i
ira tua corripias me
iserere mihi dñe qm
infirmus sum sana me
domine quoniam con
turbata sunt omnia os
sa mea et aĩa mea turba
ta est ualde Et tu dñe
usq; quo conuertere et
eripe aĩam meam saluũ
me fac propter misericõ

Plate 9: Hayes 8, Book of Hours, Gigantibus § Hayes 1, Psalter, Sanvito

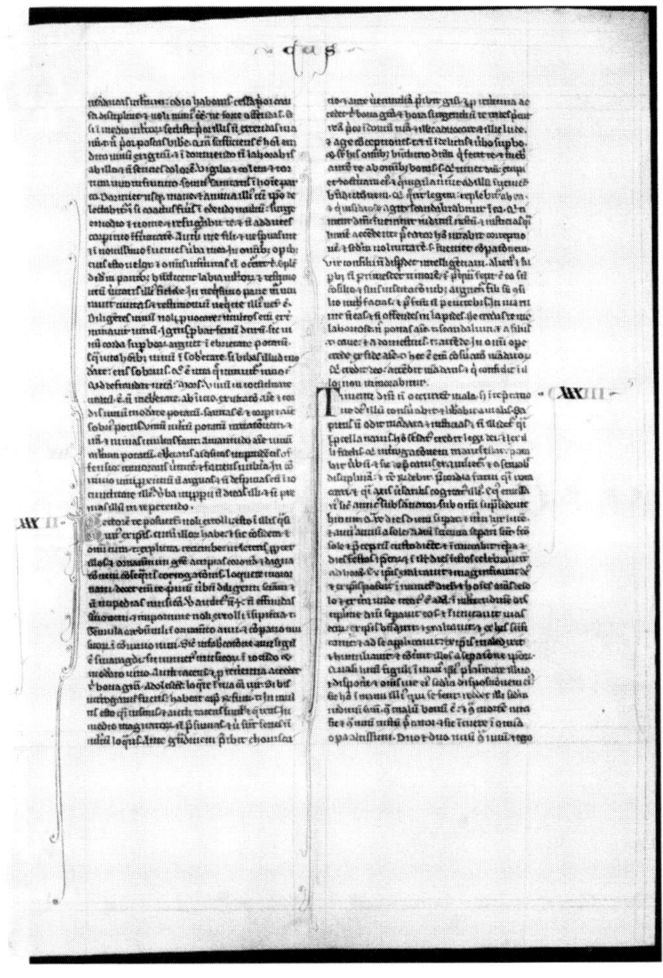

Plate 10. Ege 13, Oxford Bible

auri. Inde L. pondo data cons. et M. marcello et P.
sulpitio procons et L. ueturio pr. q̃ galliam erat
prouinciam sortitus. additumq; fabio cos. c. pondo
auri precipuum quod in arcem tarentinam portare
tur Cetero auro usi sunt ad uestimenta presenti
pecunia locanda exercitus q̃ in hispania bellu secda
sua fama ducisq; gerebat. Prodigia prius q̃ ab ur
be proficiscerentur cons procurari placuit. In alba
no monte tacto de celo erant signum iouis. arborq;
templo propinqua et hostium lacus. et capue mur
fortuneq; edes. et sinuesse murus portaq; de celo
tacta. cruentam etiam fluxisse aquam albanam
qdam auctores erant. Et rome intus in cellam
edis fortune de capite signum quod in corona e
rat in manum sua sponte prolapsum. Et priuerni
satis constabat bouem locutum uulturemq; freque
ti foro in tabnam deuolasse. et sinuesse natum am
biguo inter marem et feminam sexu infantem.
quos androginos uulgus ut pleraq; faciliore ad
duplicanda uerba greco sermone appellat. Et la
cte pluisse. et cum elephanti capite puerum nati.
E a prodigia hostiis maiorib; procurata et supplica
tio circa omnia puluinaria. et obsecratio in unum
diem indicta et decretum ut. c. hostibus pr. ludos

Plate 12. Ege 14, Bible

§

Ege 7, Aurora

Plate 13. Ege 15, Missal § MS 313, Book of Hours (fol. 49, miniature)

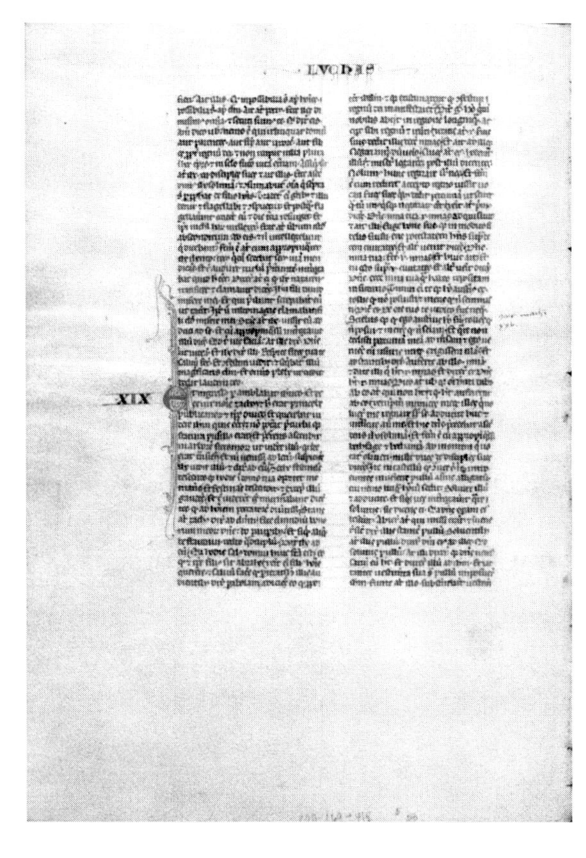

Plate 14. MS 328, The Gospel of Luke

Plate 15: MS 300, Bible